TERRAN EMPIRE

The
Genesis Project:
Bringing order to a chaotic world

First Edition

For more than 20 years Scott Yancey has been developing the Genesis Project as a viable alternative to living in today's world with a greater degree of freedom than can be obtained by the average person under today's current economic and social systems. It has been Scott's desire, for many years, to share this project with others in the hopes that they too can open doors to a much happier and free life.

Scott currently lives on Petit Jean Mountain in Conway County, Arkansas. If you would like to contact Scott about anything in this book you may do so at: **scott.yancey@terran-empire.us**. Alternatively you may take part in the discussion board devoted exclusively to the Genesis Project here:

http://genesis-project.boards.net/

Printed in the United States of America

CURRENT BOOKS OF THE EMPIRE

The Genesis Project: Bringing order to a chaotic world

FORTHCOMING BOOKS

Citizen's Handbook
The Exodus Project

TABLE OF CONTENTS

ACKNOWLEDGEMENTS

I would like to thank all of those involved with the writing of this book to include the following:

Robert Howes: for information and ideas regarding cooperatives.

DEDICATION

This book is dedicated to the people of the world, especially the homeless and those in need, the innocent people and children harmed by war, and all those who suffer at the hands of greed and corruption. May a new world be in your future where these things can no longer cause you suffering. In working together we can accomplish the great works described in this book.

FORWARD

Those that have awakened to the madness of the condition of current society and government policy find themselves outnumbered, without a voice, no one to vote for and no power to change things. Many who have awakened are separated into many different groups, thus splintering efforts and effectiveness. Banding together and uniting as one, even as communities, has advantages.

I have chosen to write this book as an attempt to express my thoughts and ideas on creating communities with an eye toward expanding into a state and to generate interest in the Terran Empire, which plans to do just that.

Scott Yancey
22 June 2017
Petit Jean Mountain, Arkansas, U.S.A.

PART I
INTRODUCTION

INTRODUCTION

Our plan for the world is ambitious; it involves nothing less than the complete transformation of society. Our desire is to end poverty, hunger, homelessness and suffering for people through our projects. We seek the unification of all people of Earth as one free people under social principles. We promote peace, the common good, the protection of our planet and its responsible steward-ship, and the advancement of science and technology in support of these goals. We hope to accomplish these things through our Genesis Project.

The Genesis Project is a community building project tasked with establishing planned communities that will eventually incorporate as cities. As such, there may be several subordinate city projects established under the Genesis Project plan. Once established, the primary objective of the Genesis Project will be territorial expansion through city building or rebuilding.

It is suggested that you somehow obtain the following books as companion books to your library. Many of the concepts discussed in these books will be utilized in our projects:

- *THE BEST THAT MONEY CAN'T BUY: Beyond Politics, Poverty and War*, by Jacque Fresco & Roxanne Meadows
- *UBUNTU Contributionism: A Blueprint for Human Prosperity*, by Michael Tellinger

CITY BUILDING PROJECTS

"Nicolai Oroussoff comes to the right conclusion: when you are trying to build a city, it's about championing the public good, not counting beans." "The fact is that great cities do not rely on cutting-edge architecture. They rely on a clear framework of streets and open spaces, designed by and for the public that over time can support the full spectrum of architecture, from the pedestrian to the heroic."

Robert Lane, Director of Design
Regional Plan Association, New York

It is our desire to establish cities that are planned and designed in such a way that they are independent and self-sufficient, concerned about environmental issues, community health and needs, where each person may advance themselves physically and intellectually.

We intend to establish our cities wherever it is feasible to do so. In order to do this, the law generally requires as a first condition that a certain number of registered voters who desire to establish a city be located in the same local area. Sometimes it is required that they must also be landholders. How are we to accomplish this? The answer can be found in a phased plan of action, each phase itself being composed of a set of objectives. This plan of action and the phases will be discussed in **PART III – MAKING THE DREAM A REALITY**. The first four phases comprise a foundation which is necessary before a city can be incorporated. The phases are as follows:

PHASE I: Community Planning
PHASE II: Obtain Land and Equipment
PHASE: III: Community Building
PHASE IV: City Planning
PHASE V: Incorporation
PHASE VI: City Building, Growth and Expansion

WHAT IS A COMMUNITY?

Before we can begin the process of community planning and building we need to have an understanding of what a community is. When someone says "community" many people will envision a place where people are tied to one another through some form of cultural bond.

The most basic unit of any community is the individual. While the individual might exist within a family or operate within some organization that functions within the community, without the individual there can be no community.

It is vitally important that responsible communities provide first for the basic needs of individuals, such as: food, shelter, clothing, medical care and a safe and secure environment. Secondly, the community must provide the means by which individuals may better themselves morally, intellectually and physically. Knowing these needs will help us understand what basic facilities and institutions must be established as priorities within our communities.

While individuals are the basic unit of a community and of the institutions and organizations that operate within it, it is the institution and organization such as the family, group, business and non-profit that are the building blocks of communities. These institutions and organizations provide the means through which life flows into the community, each providing their own unique benefits to the community as a whole.

Taken together, communities become the building blocks of cities, states and nations. With this understanding of what communities are we may now begin the process of community planning, development and building with an eye toward expansion.

PART II
IMPORTANT ISSUES

INTRODUCTION

As we plan our communities and cities there are a great many things we must consider in the process. In this part of the book we discuss many of those issues.

AGRICULTURE

Agriculture will play a vital role in the survival of the people so it should be no surprise that our society, in general, will be agrarian in nature. It only makes sense that our society produce its own crops and raise its own live-stock rather than depend on imports.

Agriculture will give us a tool for trade and will become one of the most important industries to our cities because so many products like food, medicine, textiles, fuels, building materials, etc. are derived from agriculture. Agriculture will become a major factor to our self-reliant independence because it will reduce our dependence on outside resources and allow us to eliminate contaminants accidently or deliberately placed in our food and water. What we do not use for ourselves can be used for trade and export, which will help fund government operations and government programs designed to support the people.

When considering what crops and livestock to establish in the beginning, we must first consider food staples and medicines. We must be able to provide for our own nutrition and healing and we must do so from our own soil. Second, we must consider crops used for the production of fuel for our farming implements, utility vehicles and government vehicles (which include public safety and emergency vehicles). Finally, we must consider crops and livestock for all other possible uses including clothing and other textiles, leather, paper, exports, etc. We must look at every plant and every animal for their potential uses and cultivation.

Generally crops and livestock will do well in some areas and not in others. Therefore, when considering which crops to plant and which livestock to raise, consideration should be given to climate and length of growing seasons.

When recognized for its vital importance, it becomes clear that an infrastructure supporting agriculture will be needed. Such an infrastructure must include mandatory agricultural education.

We will classify agricultural products into one of three categories depending upon its use:

- Food.
- Medicine.
- Industry.

BUILDING & CONSTRUCTION

Building and construction is a very important aspect of community building. People need places to live and places to work, places to shop and places to have fun or relax. From the building of homes and agricultural facilities to hospitals, government buildings, businesses, parks and recreational facilities, all of these make up the physical structure of our communities. To accomplish these great works, skilled labor is needed.

Recruiting is an essential part of our program. It is through recruiting that we find the skilled labor we need to accomplish our works. As we recruit those with building and construction skills, we must organize these folks into teams.

Under the operations division, building and construction teams are organized along the same lines as military units with a structured chain of command and organized according to the type of vocation. Architects, engineers and contractors might comprise the body of officers who direct the various building projects while carpenters, electricians, plumbers, painters, etc. might make up the smaller units under the leadership and command of the officers. When any structure has been determined to be needed, these teams would be deployed to make it happen.

Some structures will be standardized, as with the dwellings in a residential district. In such cases where standardization is incorporated, building and construction can be modular in nature with the structures growing only as needed according to a standard design. For example, in a residential district where a house or commonwealth has been assigned, the structures are built in a modular fashion as the family or commonwealth grows. Apartments and recreational facilities are added as they are needed.

In order to support building and construction, vocational schools must be established dedicated to building and construction trades and with standardized courses of instruction. Upon graduation, students will be assigned to a building and construction team.

COMMUNITY EVENTS

Community events are important for many reasons although primarily because they help to establish community pride and to establish stronger bonds between the individual members of the community.

Community events not only provide entertainment and recreation, they offer opportunities for socialization with the other members of the community on a larger scale in an informal environment.

Community events can be established on any of several themes, from the celebration of a season, a summertime festival, for example, to the celebration of an established holiday.

ECONOMY

Removing people from burden of debt is as the heart of our ideals. In the nations where capitalism is present, corporations and banks have no regard for people and no concept of ethical behavior. Private gain is accomplished only at the expense of one's fellow man. Money rules unchecked. It is a destructive influence to all that is natural. Profit drives greed and credit is the instrument by which a people are burdened with debt. The corporations and banks, and the people who control them, feed upon the needs and desires of the people. People in capitalist societies rush to incur debt unaware of the fact that they are being shackled by debt slavery, all the while banks and creditors take their money in the form of interest, a practice known as usury, which is income that has not been earned. Those people who have thrown themselves into interest slavery work to earn income with little reward as it is taken from them as their money pays off interest. Everyone suffers under the burden of interest payments. Yet it goes unchallenged.

Debt slavery is the condition of those who suffer under the burden of capitalism. The worker and the farmer, both who labor to produce, and the common man all live under debt slavery, while stockholders and a very few effortlessly receive huge amounts of money from banks, interest income, stocks and other financial transactions. Even a nation that borrows in order to cover its needs exists under debt slavery. The welfare of people depends upon abolishing debt slavery and keeping it from ever resurfacing to subjugate people again.

A system must be established whereby people are shielded from the negative results of capitalism. The institutions that the Terran Empire establishes must act as an economic shield for the people. These institutions will do this by interacting directly with other communities and governments that operate under capitalism. During a transitional period the Terran Empire intends to establish a system that is partially planned but that is primarily democratic through the development of the Imperial Cooperative.

In our communities people will work to produce for the needs of the community while excess product is traded by our institutions with other communities, companies and governments for materials or profit. For example, each house or commonwealth produces agricultural product. More than enough product will be produced for our own people. What excess is produced may be exported for profit or materials. Our institutions may then use that profit to purchase needed equipment or materials, or it may be traded directly for materials. Such equipment and materials may be used to set up facilities used to produce products and machinery to aid in building projects such as needed public facilities and living spaces. Perhaps some of these facilities are for the medical care of people or their education. Perhaps some are used as food processing facilities. The possibilities are many. The point here, of course, is that the profit benefits people as a whole, not just a wealthy few.

Eventually removing money from our communities will go a long way toward reducing crime and corruption because in the majority of these cases money is the single motivating factor in one way or another, either directly or indirectly. If money were removed as a motivating factor there would be no point to many types of crime or corruption.

We must also prevent commodities from becoming a form of money, circulating as do paper notes and coins. Otherwise one form of currency has simply been replaced with another. Something must be used to replace all forms of currency, whether product, banknotes or coins. What we believe would work in our case is to replace currency in whatever form with the labor-time credit.

CREDITS

In 1820 it was Robert Owen who was the first to suggest the use of labour-time vouchers in place of money. Robert Owen founded co-operative communities wherein the means of production were owned by the community in common. The people of the community produced what the community had determined was needed. In return, the people of the community who produced what the community needed were issued notes, or labor-time vouchers, certifying how many hours they had worked. The note could then be used to obtain any product or products that had taken the same amount of time to produce from the stock of community goods. The notes were not money because they didn't circulate. They were only the evidence or proof of the common labor of the individual and thus of his or her right to the same portion of the common produce for consumption.

In our case the labor-time voucher will take on the more permanent and durable form of a plastic debit card. The electronic credit will become the evidence of time worked. The credits may accumulate until used and will not circulate once spent. They are used within the context of co-operative ownership and production for use.

Before we get into a discussion of why we intend to use labor-time credits I feel it is important to explain why I have used the term "credit" in the first place. The term "credit" is not used here in the capitalist sense of the word. It is used because it represents a unit of time spent working that is "credited" to a worker's account once they've earned it.

In our case the voucher is replaced by a plastic reusable card, much like a check card. In fact it operates in the same way as a check card except that when it is used the electronic credits are not transferred to a merchant's account, they are simply deleted instead. The card itself is only a key to access the worker's account. Because the card is a reusable key, much like the metal key on a person's key ring, paper does not continually need to be produced from trees to create actual paper vouchers. The electronic credits require no ink to keep track of them. As a result the burden of demand on natural resources for these items is reduced. Damaged, lost or stolen cards can be electronically de-activated and a new card issued. Damaged cards can be recycled to make new cards or might even be used in the production of new products.

Now, having said all that, **why even bother using cards and electronic credits in the first place? Why not just give everything away for free?** In answer to these questions there is one, and only one, answer: **incentive to work**. If everyone has free access to everything what is the incentive or motivation to work? An idealist would say "because it is the right thing to do" or "because it is for the common good, the worker may receive gratification in their work." While this may be true for some people it isn't true for all people. For some, ideals are not enough. There must be something more useful and practical to the worker than ideals or you will simply end up with a shortage of workers. There wouldn't be enough workers even to produce those things to which the people would have free access. Continual shortages of the necessities of life have, in the past, caused societies to crumble and fall. We must operate with due diligence to ensure that we can provide for people's basic needs, which necessarily requires providing the workers with the necessary motivation, or incentive, to do the work that needs to be done.

As we define them, the basic needs to which everyone must have free access are food, clothing, shelter, health & medical care and safety & security. For these things no one needs to use any form of exchange to obtain them.

Ok, so the labor-time credits are the incentive or motivation for the workers to work, but how exactly? What is the need if they already have free access to the things they need? What are you supposed to do with them? In answer to these questions let's think about something for a moment. What would the quality of your life be if all you ever had was only what you needed and nothing more? What if all you had to look forward to was work and survival? Life would be very boring and unfulfilling for most people. Some people are just fine with that and have mastered the art of living simply. But I believe that the morale of the people in general would falter and the quality of their work would drop considerably. Eventually we would end up with psych patients, mostly suicide attempts, in our hospitals or, worse yet, in our morgues and graveyards. The daily lives of people would be miserable. Only some of this can be alleviated by free access to parks and some forms of recreation. However, the labor-time credits are a means by which people might access other forms of entertainment. Taking a date out to a restaurant, for example, or maybe even to a movie. Or perhaps to obtain supplies for a hobby or favorite pastime. Perhaps even to obtain items to decorate their living spaces so that they don't have to look at four plain walls every day. People not only have needs. They have wants and, while they will be provided with their needs, they must use the labor-time credits for their wants. And therein is provided the incentive and motivation to work, and the reason why we will utilize the labor-time credits as part of our economy, at least for a time.

LABOR THEORY OF VALUE

To understand how our system of credits will work it will help to have at least a basic understanding of the labor theory of value.

Labor is the basis of value and is used-up human energy. The value of a product is determined by the amount of *socially necessary* labor contained in it or, rather, by the amount of socially necessary labor-time spent producing it from start to finish. The value of a product is not determined by the *actual* amount of labor contained in it because that would mean that an inefficient or lazy worker could create more value than an efficient one. Socially necessary means the amount of labor needed to produce or reproduce a product under average working conditions, meaning average productivity and average intensity of labor. The cost of the product, then, is based on its value.

ECONOMIC TRANSITION

There are a few different types of economy throughout the world but the most prevalent of these is capitalism. Because capitalism is such a detrimental economic system to people and because the Genesis Project will be initiated under a capitalist system, transitioning from a capitalist economy to a free access society is what will be discussed here.

Jumping right into a free access society from capitalism simply isn't possible because the systems, industries and mindset that would support a free access society on a large scale do not exist today. They must first be initiated and established before a free access society can come into being. A process of transition must first occur whereby the things needed to bring about a free access society are incrementally put into place. The Terran Empire has established the following five stages of transition:

STAGE 1	Current situation in the present day – Capitalism – money / debt based – corporate and banking greed, corruption and control including control of politics and government – class based system
STAGE 2	Cooperative – money / labor based – democratic control by the workers of the work place – cooperative and workers still participate in the capitalist economy
STAGE 3	Cooperative – labor credit / labor based – cooperative still participates in the capitalist economy while workers do not
STAGE 4	Cooperative – Partial automation – fewer workers – more products and services become free access with no cost
STAGE 5	Fully automated – Capitalist economy abolished – all products and services become free access with no cost – new resource based economy is established – all are equal in a classless based society

In the beginning it may be necessary for the first community members to fully participate in the capitalist economy. However while doing so they would also start the process of establishing the system whereby they may begin to pull away from capitalism. In this beginning stage our institutions will participate more so than the individual in the capitalist economy. This is the first step in the transitional phase. Our institutions will take the place of the corporation. Rather than any profit going to a wealthy few at the top of the corporation it is applied by our institutions toward providing better community or city services for the people.

EMPLOYMENT & LABOR

Labor is the life's blood of our communities. When a person becomes old enough to work they do so for the benefit of their family and of their community. When one is working to tend the crops or livestock for which one's family or commonwealth is responsible, they contribute to the wellbeing of both their family or commonwealth and to that of the community since, through agricultural pro-duction, the people of the community have food to eat and medicines to make them well, and industry has the raw materials with which to carry on production. When one works in government, industry or a commercial environ-ment, they are producing goods and materials, providing goods and materials to the people of the community or maintaining order, safety and security within the com-munity.

Each person who works is important and vital to the community. The person who tends crops and livestock is just as important as the person who manufactures goods and materials, provides those goods and materials to the people through a commercial environment or the soldier and policeman who provide for the safety and security of the community. For the sake of the vitality of the com-munity, families and commonwealths, no profession or type of work is more important than any other. All labor is important and necessary.

An unfortunate occurrence with regard to labor are those individuals who will not perform their fair share of the labor thereby forcing their co-workers to work even harder to take up the slack. Reasonable and effective methods must be developed to work with these people that include an attempt to discover the underlying reason why the person is not effectively working. The solution may be as simple as a transfer to a different type of work or perhaps downgrading the amount of labor-time with which the worker is credited.

IMPERIAL COOPERATIVES

The cooperative will place the means of production under democratic control of the people. The aim of this is to put an end to many of the ills of society such as: poverty, hunger, unemployment, economic insecurity, war, racism and environmental crisis. These are caused as a direct result of production for profit, not production for human need. Production for human need is the key to eliminating these negative issues.

This cooperative can demonstrate democratic control of the workplace by giving the workers experience with the mechanics of workplace democracy. The cooperative will provide an opportunity to workers to prove to themselves, through their experience in the cooperative, that they simply don't need the capitalist system to sustain them or their families in any way. They learn about the negative nature of capitalism through the cooperative and their participation in it.

Although the cooperative would engage in many different trades, the highest priority of this cooperative is to produce for the basic needs of people which are defined by the Terran Empire as:

- Food
- Shelter

- Clothing
- Health & Medical Care
- Safety & Security

Because many of these needs rely on agriculture, this will be the first and foremost activity that the cooperative will engage in. Food, clothing, some building materials and medicines can all be produced from agriculture.

FOOD PRODUCTION

Food production is an essential activity of the cooperative to keep people fed and healthy. Cooperative food production is intended to be a supplemental and secondary source of food for people. Dwellings and other buildings will be designed so that food may be grown within them as part of the internal landscaping and décor, a food production source that would be available year round. External landscaping can be used for the same purpose. Regarding cooperative food production a program of fair distribution would need to be developed to ensure that each individual or family in the community would be provided with the food they need to keep them healthy and that would prevent anyone from taking an unfair advantage of the food distribution program.

Food produced in excess may be distributed in ways that help those in need and that provide a positive image of our organization and communities, and that bring attention to our projects and programs. One example promoted by Robert Howes would be to open a free café that is stocked with the produce we have in excess. Anyone who is hungry would be invited to eat in the café for free. In our case, the café would be managed by the community (or city). It would be important to have literature freely available to the café patrons about all of the things we wish to promote.

Examples of such materials might include table cards, business cards, flyers, placemats, wall posters, brochures, information included on menus and even audio programming played within the café, mixing both music and spoken media. In some cases talks may be provided explaining what we do and why with a question and answer session following the talk.

Another example might include the distribution of food boxes to those in need. These food boxes could be distributed to local aid agencies as well as distributed out directly to those in need. Food boxes would include some of the information about our organization, projects and programs like that of the information that would be provided in the café.

CLOTHING PRODUCTION

Agriculture would support clothing production. The cooperative would produce clothing and other textiles that would be provided to people for free according to their need. Clothing might also be produced and provided free to those in need through a program similar to that of the food box distribution program mentioned above with the associated informational materials. Some clothing might be provided for purchase through our café or through our market in order to raise funds.

MEDICINAL PREPARATIONS

The cooperative would produce medicinal preparations from agricultural produce that would be provided to people for free when needed. Some of those preparations might be made available for sale, as supplements, through our market or through our free café's. The distribution and dispensing of certain preparations may depend on the type and use for the preparation. Ideally our communities will have their own clinics and, eventually, hospitals.

SHELTER

The need for shelter can only be partially supported by agriculture. Other materials will be needed that we cannot produce for ourselves in the beginning. Eventually, however, the production of lumber can be handled internally, which would require the planting, and replanting, of trees as a crop. Unfortunately, it would take many years for trees to mature to the point where they could be used to produce lumber. Other methods of building that do not rely on lumber so much will have to be pursued. One example would be to utilize hemp as a building material as well as ICF's (Insulated Concrete Forms).

EDUCATION & CULTURE

Education is necessary for a youth to become an empowered and productive person. This not only helps the youth, but also the community as a whole. The youth of today become the leaders of tomorrow. It is important that youth are brought up from a very young age in social ideals that promote the common good and that they are instructed and well trained to become honest, loyal and productive people.

Left idle and lacking in direction, youth tend to find ways to get into trouble. It becomes important to structure a youth's time with positive and productive activity throughout each day.

The first of these activities is education. The first part of the day for each youth is dedicated to education. After the educational part of the day youth should be involved in after school activities within a boys or girls youth organization. These two organizations have the primary responsibility of instructing boys and girls, young men and women, in their roles as productive people in our communities. The activities offered by these organizations would include athletic and sports activities, hiking, camping, first aid and CPR, instruction in the arts, crafts and other hobbies.

EDUCATION

Facilities must be constructed to support education and cultural development. Such facilities may include:

- School buildings
- Libraries
- Museums
- Art galleries
- City cultural centers

EDUCATIONAL SAFETY

Considering the rash of public school violence that has been occurring in recent times it should come as no surprise that the safety of our children is our number one priority. Our children should be protected from violence in schools. Such violence has ranged from shootings and explosive devices to bullying that has, in turn, resulted in retaliatory violence. Our schools must be safe institutions of learning for our children.

There are two main areas to discuss when considering educational safety and these are the architectural designs of the buildings and the policies, procedures and training of both students and staff.

ARCHITECTURAL DESIGNS

The school buildings and even to a greater degree the school campuses must be designed in such a way as to promote learning and imagination while still promoting the safety and security of staff, students and visitors. These should be built as highly secured and safe areas without feeling like stifling prisons.

Some of the features that these buildings and campuses may include are parameter access barriers, security camera systems, on site security and medical personnel, on site clinics, access control systems and metal detection systems. Other features may include restricted access areas based on whether one is a student, staff or visitor. These features must work hand in hand with the established policies, procedures and training of the facility.

POLICIES, PROCEDURES & TRAINING OF STUDENTS AND STAFF

In establishing the policies, procedures and training of our educational institutions it must be understood that safety, security and education must come first and convenience second. The safety and security standards must be in place and enforced and upheld by all staff members jointly. Certain staff members will play key roles with regard to more specific areas of the policies, procedures and training of these institutions.

Some policies, procedures and training will be standardized across all educational facilities while others may be more specific and specialized to a particular facility as needs require.

ENTERTAINMENT

We must provide forms of entertainment to the people of our communities which may include anything from sporting events to concerts, plays and movies. Our people may form intercity sports teams that compete with one another. Cities may establish their own teams and compete with other cities. Community members and cities might form bands, orchestras, acting guilds, etc. Our cities must consider providing community members with facilities and support for these activities which might include sports arenas, concert and music halls, play houses and studios.

SPORTS

Various sports facilities can be established for the different sports. A suggested list of the first sports established would be:

- Soccer
- Football
- Baseball
- Basketball
- Tennis
- Hockey
- Wrestling
- Kickball

This is not an exhaustive list and other sports in addition to these may be established later.

ORPHANAGES

Our institutions must maintain orphanages for those children who have lost their family and have no house or commonwealth to care for them. The orphanages must be warm and caring environments for children where our ideals are constantly reinforced. Where possible, existing houses or families within a commonwealth may adopt children from the orphanages.

ADMINISTRATION

The administration is only a managing entity for the people. It exists for the maintenance of the people, which is the one principle that must remain throughout its existence. The people are the primary thing. Everything else is secondary. If the agencies of a government are not able to fulfill this one thing, their existence cannot be justified. They must be reformed or replaced as the case may be. Something more efficient and better must take its place.

Individuals make up families, commonwealths and organizations. Families, commonwealths and organizations are the foundation of community, and communities are the building blocks of the state. Governments are not to exist to oppress the people. Nor are they to exist simply to expand their own power and control or to do the bidding of other organizations or institutions who wish to subjugate, control and ultimately burden, or enslave, the people. Governments are given authority to manage the affairs of society so that the best interests of the people are served. The people are best served when their basic needs are met. This essentially includes keeping the peace, homeland expansion, national defense, etc. It is the responsibility of governments, as an agent of the people, to ensure that these needs are met to the best of its ability. Ultimately, this is the only reason for governments to exist.

Only a government can hope to accomplish the acquisition of a homeland and to further protect it and its people through the orderly management of the appropriate resources (including raw materials, equipment, etc.), that are obtained from the communities as a whole. Government or, in our case, the administration has better and greater access to resources than does one or two organizations.

While it is not currently possible to establish a state government, it is possible to establish elements of a functioning administration in the form of non-profit organizations. When we establish a city, we become much closer to realizing our goals.

It should be understood that as the cities are established they still must operate under the laws of the higher jurisdictions under which they exist. The point, however, is to start small locally and expand until those higher jurisdictions become our own.

ENACTING LAW

The administration must be prohibited, in every aspect, from creating, voting on, enacting or repealing laws. This must be the exclusive right of the people. If this privilege were ever given to a government, even if in a representative or congressional form, they will eventually use their privilege to burden the people with debt and support special interests, as we can see being done today.

In the past a representative form of government may have not been perfect but was the most practical form of government under the circumstances at that time. Today, however, we possess the technology where each person may participate directly in the process of law and administration from the comfort of their homes without relying on representatives or even political parties. Each person can freely vote their conscience without the pressure of some political group. The problem with representatives is that they can be influenced by special interest groups whose interests may not be in *your* best interest or in that of the people.

SECULAR ADMINISTRATION

Because of the many different belief systems of the people, or lack thereof, the foundation of our administration must necessarily be secular law and service to the people. Law, as established by the people, establishes the acceptable social standard of conduct. The law is the will of the people. It will be the job of our administration to enforce those laws, and in so doing the will of the people, so that a safe environment for our people is maintained through peace and order. No religion can be the foundation of our administration. Unfortunately, religion is one of the very things that divide us as a people.

Here in the United States there is a lot of argument and controversy regarding the separation of church and state. Because our administration must be secular in nature while still providing for the right of the people to believe whatever they wish, a discussion of these controversial issues is warranted. It is not the intent of the Terran Empire to prevent the spiritual freedom of the people which necessarily also includes one's right not to believe in any religion or form of spirituality. However, the religious beliefs of people may not be allowed to influence our administration.

ONE PLANETARY ADMINISTRATION

The Terran Empire does advocate one planetary administration. Today, all across the planet, we are a people divided. If we, as humans, wish to truly be free we must work together to limit or even remove the things that divide us, that limit our possibilities and that prevent us from achieving our greatest potential. Government and politics are two of the things that divide us. All world governments should be consolidated into one planetary administration and limited to the purpose of governance as described herein. Politics should be eliminated completely.

HOMELESSNESS

Homelessness, essentially, is the condition of an individual or a family being without proper shelter (a home) and is the result of the failure of several social systems. Homelessness has no place in a responsible community. Each and every cause of homelessness must be addressed and countered. The first and foremost solution to homelessness is the establishment of a house or a commonwealth, which is the first step in establishing a permanent home for an individual or family, and assigning that house or commonwealth to a residential district.

It is absolutely insane that people and families are homeless because they cannot afford a home, while so many foreclosed homes sit empty. In part, homelessness is caused by a profit motive in the real estate and banking industries. In this Genesis Project plan, families are provided with a home and there is no need to be homeless. There is no profit motive involved here.

Another cause of homelessness is mental illness, which is not appropriately addressed in our profit driven medical *industry*. The practice of medicine MUST put people before profit. The Genesis Project plan does exactly that by removing the profit motive altogether through the use of the LTC system, bringing medicine back to the purpose of care and healing rather than making money.

PROBLEMS FACED BY THE HOMELESS

Some of the problems faced by the homeless are:

- Meeting the basic human needs, which are literally vital.
- Personal security, quiet and privacy, especially for sleeping.
- Safekeeping of clothing, bedding and possessions, which may have to be carried at all times.
- Hygiene and sanitary facilities.
- Cleaning and drying of clothes.
- Obtaining, preparing and storing food in quantities.
- Keeping contacts, without a permanent location or mailing address.
- Hostility and legal powers against urban vagrancy.

Just by providing living space in a residential district, ALL of these problems are alleviated. But there are also other problems beyond the lack of a suitable living space. Socially the homeless are faced with reduced access to private and public services and reduced access to vital necessities such as:

- Access to health care and dental services.
- Limited access to education.
- Increased risk of suffering from violence and abuse.
- General rejection or discrimination from others.
- Loss of usual relationships with the mainstream.
- Not being seen as suitable for employment.
- Reduced access to communications technology.

Many of these issues are addressed by built-in solutions within the Genesis Project, the first of which is through providing living space and basic needs, and the second is ensuring that everyone who wants to work is able to do so. Many times it is a profit motive that *prevents* employers from hiring new employees.

Due to the way society is to be recreated through the Genesis Project and it's built in systems and services, the need for assistance organizations can eventually be eliminated and absorbed into our own institutions. Some of these institutions and organizations may even choose to opt into, and become integrated into, our Genesis Project plan.

INDUSTRY

Industry is generally classified into four and some-times five sectors. Understanding these classifications may help when we begin the development of our communities. These sectors are as follows:

PRIMARY SECTOR

The primary sector includes farming, logging and mining. This sector involves extracting resources directly from the Earth. Industries in the primary sector do not process the materials they extract. The raw materials are sent to the secondary sector for processing.

SECONDARY SECTOR

The secondary sector is involved in the processing of raw materials from the industries of the primary sector. This sector generally includes all factories.

TERTIARY SECTOR

The tertiary sector is involved in providing services and includes service providers, teachers, medical care, etc.

QUARTERNARY SECTOR

The quaternary sector is involved in the research and development of science and technology. This sector is composed primarily of scientists.

QUINARY SECTOR

Sometimes a fifth sector is included called the quinary sector that includes domestic activities performed by stay-at-home parents and homemakers.

The first industries in our communities must be those that are related to basic needs and that support our community and the basic needs of people. Foremost among these industries will be agriculture, for which established houses and commonwealths will be responsible. Agriculture will meet the basic needs of food, shelter, clothing and medicine. Agriculture can also produce fuels for our farming implements and specialized vehicles (ambulances, police vehicles, fire engines, construction vehicles, etc.)

The next set of industries to follow agriculture would be industries that transform agricultural produce into the things that meet our basic needs. These might include food processing plants, textiles plants, building construction and pharmaceutical plants. With regard to pharmaceuticals, without a profit motive driving pharmaceutical development, medications would be developed that treat causes rather than just symptoms.

After these industries others may follow as they are needed.

PARKS & RECREATION

Various types of parks and recreation help to improve the quality of life of people on several levels. They encourage exercise and learning and promote health and mental well being. Ideally, a park should utilize an entire district although in some cases they may be incorporated into other districts in various ways.

Parks may be:

- Theme parks
- Zoos
- Aquariums
- Playgrounds
- Open green spaces

Recreation might include:

- Sports fields and arenas
- Bike trails
- Hiking trails
- Boating marinas and docks

PUBLIC HEALTH

Public health includes both sanitation and medical concerns.

WASTE MANAGEMENT

It is inevitable and natural that we produce waste. It simply cannot be avoided. Therefore, responsible waste management becomes an important duty and responsibility of every individual and organization within our communities. There are many reasons for responsible waste management. Among them are health, reduction of pollution (which in turn affects not only the health of people but the health of the environment that supports us), and beautification of our lands and communities just to name a few.

There are several kinds of waste but two primary categories are that which is biodegradable and that which is not. Also, these wastes can be classified as hazardous wastes and non-hazardous wastes.

RECYCLING PROGRAMS

Recycling programs can incorporate the recycling of both biodegradable waste and non-biodegradable wastes. Organic waste products can be recycled into fertilizer and other biodegradable products, such as cardboard and paper, or they can be recycled into new products.

Non-organic wastes, like plastic containers (necessary to preserve the freshness of foods in order to prevent illnesses), can be recycled into new products for re-use.

Recycling reduces the amount of garbage that will go into landfills, keeping subsequent pollution and land requirements minimal.

MEDICAL FACILITIES

Hospitals and clinics must be made available to people and for that purpose administrative districts will be established and dedicated specifically to medical uses. Each administrative medical district would include a children's hospital, general hospital, geriatric hospital and a psychiatric hospital. Medical clinics that specialize in specific medical disciplines and medical research facilities would also be located in administrative medical districts.

The four types of hospitals will make one concentric ring around the district center. Outside of that another concentric ring will be composed of various types of clinics. Outside of that another concentric ring will be composed of medical research facilities.

PUBLIC SAFETY

Public safety includes emergency services such as police, fire departments and ambulance services as well as other safety related organizations. Safety related organizations should be created by our administrative institutions to ensure the safety of the people while working or while simply going about their daily lives. These safety organizations must be responsible for establishing protocols, procedures and safety standards in various environments.

PUBLIC HOUSING INTAKE

A public housing intake district will need to be established in our first city to accommodate those who wish to migrate to our communities. The district will be composed of apartments where individuals and families will live until they can be placed in a regular public housing district if they are single individuals, couples, or couples with children. Families will be organized into a house or given the opportunity to join a commonwealth and will remain in public housing until a residential district or place in a commonwealth becomes available.

As part of the migration and intake program, we must facilitate transportation projects that assist individuals and families to get to our intake processing districts.

FAMILY

We believe that an organized family will function more efficiently to care for its members and to produce for the community. For this reason some families will be organized into a "house."

A house is essentially the whole of a family related by blood and those to whom they are joined in union, as with marriage or some other similar union. A house is managed by a council of elders and, along with the commonwealth, is primarily responsible for agriculture within our communities. It stands to reason that the larger the family the more easily manageable the agricultural responsibilities of the house will be.

A "house hold" or simply a "hold" is the residential district to which the house has been assigned. Depending on the size of the family, the house may occupy more than one hold. Each portion of a house that occupies a hold is considered to be a clan. How many clans a house has depends on how many holds the house occupies. Only one clan may occupy a single residential district/hold. Many newly created houses will only start off with a single very small clan.

The house has a lot in common with the commonwealth in that they are also based upon shared cooperative activity as described on the next page.

THE COMMONWEALTH

The commonwealth is an alternative to the house structure and accepts families of all kinds, whether related by blood or not. Commonwealths are small communities in and of themselves because they are based on shared cooperative activity which is something not often seen locally in today's society. Under capitalism individualistic values are intensified due to separated living areas where neighbors hardly know one another. When this occurs community breaks down and becomes non-existent.

Our society will thrive where true community exists, where people cooperate and work together toward the common good. In order for communities to exist they need institutions that bring people together to meet real needs in ways that are better than what capitalism can provide. The Terran Empire was created for this purpose and this is what the Terran Empire attempts to do.

As with a house, a commonwealth will have agricultural responsibilities to the community and eventually to the city. It is expected that a commonwealth will become large enough that not all who live in the commonwealth will be required or needed to fulfill the agricultural requirements and responsibilities. Some of these folks may work within the commonwealth in other capacities filling some useful need while others may work elsewhere within the township or city.

POPULATION

During our period of growth and expansion, a large population is required. Politically, the larger the voting population the stronger our political voice and voting power. Through these we can influence areas to our benefit. When we have accomplished our goals we will no longer need to operate in the political arena. As such we can begin to work on population reduction through educational programs. This is what we are striving for.

RENEWABLE ENERGY & RESOURCES

Renewable energy & resources include the use of solar power and heating, hydropower, wind generated power, bio fuels and hydrogen fuels. Use of these resources by our communities helps to promote non-polluting technologies and the ability to sustain the power and other utility needs of our communities.

ENERGY

Energy classifications include energy production & collection, energy storage, energy conversion & distribution, and energy conservation.

ENERGY PRODUCTION & COLLECTION

We have at our disposal many ways to collect and produce energy. Our preferred method of energy production and collection would be to use technologies that do not pollute the environment. Such technologies would include solar, wind generated, hydro and geothermal. But these are not the only methods. There are ways to collect gases from decaying matter, and electronic devices that we can develop that tap into both man-made and natural ambient electromagnetic energy. The later devices are readily available to us as they can be constructed from scrap materials and discarded electronic devices that are either obsolete or no longer working. Electronics like Televisions and computers are sometimes simply thrown out on the curb or in the dumpster. Not all of the electronic components would be bad and could be harvested and reused in other devices. Harvesting these devices from the trash does the environment good.

It will become very important to spend some time researching and developing ways to produce energy and fuels, as with fuel from water.

GENERAL	DETAILED	USAGE / FACILITIES/DIVISIONS
Utilities	Energy	Production & Collection
		Storage
		Conversion & Distribution
		Conservation
	Water	Collection
		Processing
		Storage
		Conservation
		Distribution
	Communication	Radio / Television
		Cable / Satellite
		Internet
		Telephone
		Print

TABLE II – 2

Solar energy collection uses PV modules that convert sunlight into electricity. A solar array is a collection of PV modules that are interconnected. Sometimes solar arrays are mounted on trackers that follow the path of the sun throughout the day so that the solar arrays always directly face the sun, allowing the maximum amount of energy to be collected.

Wind generated power collects energy from the wind, converting it into electrical power. When the wind flows past a wind turbine it pushes the blades of the turbine causing it to turn a motor in the turbine housing. The motor then creates electrical energy that is stored and distributed in the same way as with solar power.

Hydroelectric power works on the same principle as wind generated power but in this case it is water that flows past the blades of a turbine rather than wind. Usually a constant flow of water at a certain flow rate is required to make hydropower practical.

ENERGY STORAGE

Electrical energy is usually stored in batteries for later use. While some devices produce enough energy to power devices directly, it is more efficient to store energy for later use when needed. Charge controllers are often used between the energy collection and production devices and the battery banks in order to prevent overcharging and damage to the batteries.

ENERGY CONVERSION & DISTRIBUTION

Batteries produce direct current (DC) electrical energy but, because most household appliances use alternating current (AC), the DC current must be converted into AC current before it can be used. This is accomplished with the use of devices called inverters. Inverters take the DC current from the batteries and produce utility grade AC electrical power from it.

How energy is distributed depends on the system for which it is used. Since inverters supply electrical current like that supplied by utility companies the distribution of the electrical current is no different than it would be in a building supplied by the utility company. However, some appliances are designed to use, and are more efficient using, direct current. Separate circuits, along with their own separate circuit breaker boxes, are needed in the building for direct current use and special outlets can be used in place of normal outlets for direct current.

ENERGY CONSERVATION

Energy conservation is important because renewable power systems do have a limited capacity that depends upon how many good batteries are used in the system. Batteries only store so much energy. If you use up all the energy stored in a battery, there is no more that can be used and you would have to do without until you can collect more. Phantom loads and equipment, appliances or lights left on when not in use drain your batteries of power. Good conservation habits can help prevent this. This means turning off lights and equipment when not in use. Appliances and equipment should be chosen that use less energy and that are energy efficient in the system so that they make the best use of power while still supplying power needs. Sometimes using devices like timer switches can help too. In some cases, though, this isn't enough.

Sometimes phantom loads can still drain the power system regardless of good conservation habits or appliance efficiency. An example of a phantom load would be a microwave with a clock built into it. Even though the microwave may be off and not in use, the clock still drains power from the batteries. It is best that these devices are plugged into switched power strips or switched wall outlets so that they can be completely switched off when not in use, depriving the phantom load of power.

WATER

Water classifications include water collection, water processing, water storage, water conservation, water distribution and uses for water.

WATER COLLECTION

Water is a basic need for life and there are many ways to collect it. In some areas however, water collection is highly regulated or even restricted. We must work to ease these regulations and restrictions in whatever way we can so that water can become an abundant resource for all people.

Water covers three-quarters of our planet and, with global warming, the melting ice caps and rising sea levels, that water coverage will only increase threatening many islands and coastal cities. In spite of this many areas still experience drought, water regulation and water restrictions.

We have the technology and manpower to help alleviate some of the issues caused by the rising sea levels as well as helping to alleviate droughts and the scarcity of water that leads to water regulation and restriction. Cost is the major prohibitive factor preventing this from being done, so it must fall to the Imperial Cooperatives to accomplish the required works. The first, and best way, to alleviate these problems is the collection and processing of sea water, of which there is a great abundance, and delivering it in various ways to the areas where it is needed. The byproducts of desalinization can also be used so there is a bonus in that process.

Where there is no drought or scarcity of water it can be collected in any number of ways and processed for drinking and agriculture. For example, water can be collected from lakes, streams, rivers and reservoirs. It can also be collected from snow, rainfall and atmospheric water generators. In some places it can even be collected from natural springs.

WATER PROCESSING

Water processing includes the activities and processes required to make water drinkable, useful for agriculture and usable in many other ways. These would include desalinization, filtration, distillation and sterilization. In some cases, even the byproducts of these processes can be useful, as with the sea salt produced from the desalinization of sea water.

WATER STORAGE

Water can be stored in reservoirs and tanks of various kinds for use when needed.

USES FOR WATER

Water has many uses, the most obvious being for drinking, cooking, cleaning and hygiene. Water is also used for medicine, scientific research and industry. It has uses in producing energy in various ways and can even be used to fuel vehicles once they are properly designed to use water as a fuel in both electric vehicles and combustion engines (using hydrogen produced from water). In space programs, both oxygen and hydrogen, produced from the electrolysis of water, are used at rocket fuels.

MEDIA & COMMUNICATION

Media & communication classifications include radio, television, cable and satellite services, internet, phone systems, print media, etc. These services could be provided through the cooperative of the communities.

SELF-SUFFICIENCY

Whereas establishing communities is the primary goal of the Terran Empire, the self-sufficiency of our communities becomes a second goal after establishing our first community. One could even go as far to say that self-sufficient practices are analogous to those goals because they can be put into practice during our struggle to achieve them.

We cannot build our future on international help. We cannot build it upon the assurances of foreign statesmen or governments. Therefore, self-sufficient practices will become of extreme importance on many levels, from the individual on up to the highest government branches. It will become a way of life for our people.

Self-sufficiency is just one tool to free a people and a nation from debt slavery. Its practice frees individuals, communities, and on a larger scale, state and government, from financial obligations that many people and governments suffer from today. One of the important points to understand about self-sufficient practices is that, when practiced by the state, it helps enforce and support the state's sovereignty, as it is not obligated to outside influences in return for aid.

TECHNOLOGY

While keeping up to date with modern technology, we need to get back to the basics of living. Technology is a wonderful tool that was meant to make life better and to enrich the lives of people. Unfortunately, due to capitalist influence and profit motive, much technology has been developed and produced to make our people dependent. We do believe that technology has value and we embrace those technologies that do what they are meant to do; enrich lives and make life easier. All current technologies should be evaluated for their practical value.

Technology for us should have the following points in common:

- They must be safe to use.
- They must enrich the lives of people without making them dependent.
- They must be classified according to their purpose and uses.

We must establish government districts dedicated to the development of specific technologies.

RESEARCH & DEVELOPMENT

While it's true that money can enable many types of research, more often than not it is a lack of money that prevents many types of beneficial research and development from occurring. In most cases money that is invested today into research and development is usually invested by those with a profit motive into technologies that harm the environment in many ways and that makes people dependent upon those technologies. These investments are made with a profit motive in mind and not the well being of one's fellow man.

Things don't have to be this way. The key is to remove money from the equation. When money is not a factor and the resources are available for research and development we can develop beneficial technologies that had been previously ignored. Without the interference of the profit motive a good deal of progress can be made in directions that actually help people and our planet.

ROBOTICS & AUTOMATION

In moving toward a future where fewer people have to work and where more people can simply enjoy life, it becomes obvious that robotics and automation will become one major industry in and of itself. This subject deserves much discussion and planning. It is also evident that we will need to recruit those who have an interest in or experience with robotics and automation. We must encourage them to invent and develop systems that will become useful in our future.

In determining what systems we must first consider for automation we need to look to our defined basic needs for guidance. These basic needs are primary before everything else and so should be the first considered for automation. We may not be able to automate every aspect of industry or service related to the basic needs, as with some health care issues, but as much as can be automated should be so that people won't have to spend their time working to produce for basic needs, yet the basic needs will still be provided for. Automation is one required step in moving toward a free access society.

When considering robotics and automation it becomes important to classify the areas of intended automation as well as to determine the specific job types within each area that can or cannot be automated either partially or fully. Some of these general classifications follow.

AGRICULTURAL AUTOMATION

Considering the fact that the layout of residential districts will be standardized it is reasonable to assume that automated systems can be developed to work within this framework of standardization for the production of crops and care of livestock. With regard to crops this system could be completely automated preparing the land for planting, planting the crops, watering, fertilizing and deploying pest and weed control, and even harvesting the crops. Similar systems might be implemented for livestock.

Agricultural product would then be sent to processing plants for processing and distribution according to its purpose. Here, too, automation and robotics can be implemented to a large degree.

BUILDING CONSTRUCTION

Many buildings will be standardized in design and because of this standardization automated systems can be developed that could be deployed to a site to begin the process of site preparation and building construction under human supervision and control. As these systems become more refined and developed the building process can occur more efficiently and quickly. With fewer people involved directly in the construction process there is less of a chance for injury or death for workers.

INDUSTRIAL AUTOMATION

Earlier in this book we presented a discussion regarding labor-time credits and incentive to work. With the use of labor-time credits it becomes obvious that, in the beginning, not all things would be free access. Whereas the basic needs are free access, other items and services are not. The only reason for this situation to exist is to motivate people to work. It should be understood that this is meant only to be a temporary situation. As more industries within our cities become fully automated, people will no longer need to work to produce those goods. In such cases the products of automation could then be released to become free access. People would then no longer need to use their labor-time credits to obtain those products. Ideally we would keep automating so that more and more products, and eventually all products, become free access.

ARTIFICIALLY INTELIGENT ROBOTIC COMPANIONS

One area of robotics and automation that should be given consideration is the subject of artificially intelligent robotic companions, also known as androids (or "droids"). These can be of any design, customizable and incredibly lifelike. They can be very useful to the elderly, disabled or to those who simply do not enjoy social interaction. Some models can even be designed for romance and intimacy for those who have no desire for or who have difficulty in relationships.

With regard to the elderly and disabled, androids can assist in many ways, for example, they may assist with meals, medication, hygiene, first aid and safety. They could even be programmed to summon emergency services when needed. Besides all these they can provide simple companionship and conversation. They might even be able to access information via a national intranet.

TERRITORIAL EXPANSION

There are various methods of territorial expansion available to our communities and any one of them, or combination of them can be used at any given time under the appropriate circumstances.

LAND DONATIONS

The Terran Empire will accept donations of land for use in the Genesis Project with or without structures already existing upon the land.

LAND PURCHASE

The Terran Empire may purchase land where a community may be established under the Genesis Project and will also accept financial donations and grants for this purpose.

FREE LAND PROGRAMS IN SMALL TOWNS

Free land programs present a unique opportunity for the Terran Empire. Sometimes small towns that are struggling financially will offer free lots within their town in order entice people to move to their town and build a home or start a business upon the free lot. The purpose of this is to generate greater revenue for the small town or city through taxation.

When we find towns that are offering free land, our members may take advantage of the offer by claiming lots and assisting one another in the construction of their homes. This would provide the Terran Empire with a very quick way to concentrate our members in a small local area and would also allow us to take advantage of the voting process, voting our own members into political positions of authority so that we can proceed with our city planning, building and expansion objectives within the Genesis Project.

SUBDIVISION HOME PURCHASES

Where funds permit, homes in subdivisions may be purchased. The subdivisions targeted would be those where the cost of the homes would be low. Home purchase would be concentrated in one subdivision until all homes in that subdivision have been obtained.

We would rent these homes exclusively to our own members for a very low rate, perhaps $50 to $100 a month and allowing the first two to three months to be free. This period of free rent would allow residents to have time to find income. In cases where income is difficult to find other options may be made available. This would help alleviate fears associated with relocation to a new area and encourage more migration to our specific areas. This is important in order to expand our political power base in the local area and priming the political climate for community building according to our ideals. The rents would enable us to purchase more homes.

Our goal in this method is to obtain more territory, bit by bit, in preparation for the implementation of the Genesis Project in the local area. One benefit to this method is the displacement of crime and urban decay as we progress from one subdivision to the next.

ANNEXATION AND EMINENT DOMAIN

Annexation is a legal process whereby a city may incorporate new territory within its borders. Eminent domain (also known as compulsory purchase, resumption/compulsory acquisition or expropriation) is a legal process whereby a city may use privately held land. In the case of eminent domain the city or acquiring entity must provide just compensation of the land acquired to the owner of that land. In our case we may also offer those individuals a place within our cities by assigning a resident-ial district to them or housing them in some other way if they accept our offer.

Cities established by the Genesis Project or other-wise integrated into the project, will make use of these two processes to expand our territory and to transfer privately held property over to the city for district zoning.

TRANSPORTATION

Transportation can be divided into the following categories: land, water, air and space.

LAND TRANSPORTATION

Land transportation includes motor vehicles, bicycles, electric bicycles and monorail systems. This category also includes the infrastructures that support these vehicle types such as roads, trails and guide ways. Another form of transportation in this category does not require a vehicle but refers to walking, jogging or running and would include pedestrian walkways for this purpose.

MOTOR VEHICLES

Our cities will be car free. Removing motor vehicles from the community has some very distinct advantages. Among these are low or no noise and air pollution from vehicle traffic and no vehicle accidents which usually result in serious injury, death, pain, suffering, emotional distress and immense financial loss. Also, fewer wildlife or pet fatalities caused by motor vehicles.

Due to the design of the city, the motor vehicle no longer becomes necessary to living one's day to day life and to working. We hope that eventually motor vehicles will no longer be needed for long distance travel as our cities grow.

PUBLIC TRANSPORTATION

Districts are designed with the physical health of the citizen and the environment in mind. Except in special circumstances, as with public safety and emergency vehicles, motor vehicles are not allowed in any of the districts. The district is just small enough to travel on foot or by riding a bicycle. The citizen must walk or ride a bike to travel within the district and therefore receives the health benefits of exercise.

Because travel from one district to another might involve distances that are greater than practical for walking or riding a bike, free public transportation in the form of monorail will eventually be provided. The diagram on the next page illustrates how a public transportation system will be arranged.

Forms of long distance travel must be considered as well for those traveling outside our cities, such as airports, space ports, bus depots (at the outer edge of our cities) and train stations.

Our public transportation routes are intended to be serviced by monorail, or more specifically, maglev monorail. Defined, "monorail" means a single rail serving as a track for passenger or freight vehicles. In most cases the rail is elevated but can also run at grade (or ground level), below grade or in subway tunnels. Vehicles are either suspended from or straddle a narrow guideway. Monorail vehicles are wider than the guideway that supports them.

The term "Maglev" is derived from "magnetic levitation." Maglev monorails use magnetic levitation to suspend, guide and propel vehicles from magnets as opposed to mechanical methods. Magnets create lift and

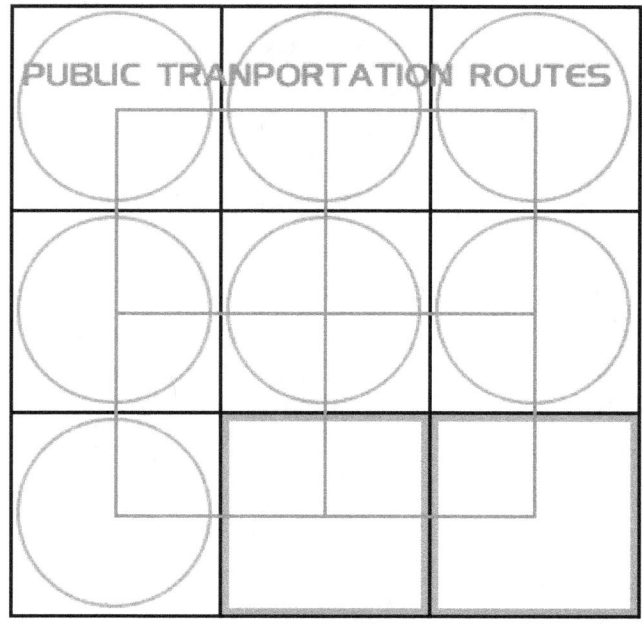

FIG. III – 1

thrust. They run more smoothly and quietly, and are capable of traveling much faster than traditional rail (some capable of reaching aircraft speeds). Maglev monorail requires less maintenance than other traditional forms of wheeled public transportation systems because there is no surface contact with the guideway. The maglev monorail floats a few inches above the track due to the magnetic forces involved. There are no friction points to cause wear. These are vehicles that essentially "fly" at very low altitude and the ride is very smooth.

Our system will have elevated guideways because they will be much safer for both people and for wild or domesticated animals. The elevated guideways will allow people and animals to pass underneath without fear of being hit by the monorail. Also, those vehicles that are allowed within the city will not be impeded by the elevated railways as they, too, may pass under the guideways. Emergency vehicles will not have to be concerned about collisions with the monorail nor will they have to sit and wait for the monorail to pass before proceeding, which could save lives. Potentially fatal accidents are also prevented by limiting stops, boarding, and disembarking to the satiations located at each district center.

Due to the fact that each district center will have a monorail station there is virtually no area of the city that a citizen could not get to. In many bus or rail systems, stops are limited and sometimes far and few between. Also, many traditional stops are located outside in the weather and during adverse weather conditions, if a person wants to catch the bus or light rail, if those are even running, they have to wait in the rain, snow, or heat, as the case may be. Most stations in our system would be protected and sheltered because most of the time they will be located within buildings.

Compared to heavy or light rail systems, construction of monorail guideways takes less time and does not prohibit movement of people and access to buildings for long periods of time. Rather than having to construct railways on the spot, the guideways and pylons can be constructed and produced off site, trucked in to the site and set up relatively quickly. To put it in simple terms, you dig a hole, place your prebuilt pylon then lift the track into place. Generally, with the right equipment, the track can be moved from truck bed to pylons in a matter of minutes.

Stations and tracks can be designed to match the surrounding environment. They do not have to be ugly constructions but can be designed to be aesthetically pleasing, or unobtrusive in green space environments. The routes can also be landscaped with various forms of plant life. Correctly designed, the tracks and pylons can help to enliven certain environments and help to create pleasant spaces and moods.

EMERGENCY, ADMINISTRATIVE & UTILITY VEHICLES

There are some activities that cannot be carried out through the use of public transportation and do, therefore, require the use and implementation of specialized vehicles. Examples would include: ambulances, fire engines, police vehicles, military vehicles, construction vehicles and other utility vehicles. Roads will be constructed around each district to facilitate movement of these vehicles and each district will be required to have an entrance and exit road to provide access to these vehicles when needed.

WATER TRANSPORTATION

Water transportation includes all vessels designed to be operated in or upon bodies of water including streams, rivers, lakes and larger open bodies of water such as bays, gulfs, seas and oceans. The infrastructures included in this category would include shipyards, docks, marinas and ports.

AIR TRANSPORTATION

Air transportation includes all vessels designed to float or fly in the air and the infrastructures designed to support air transportation such as airports and landing strips.

SPACE TRANSPORTATION

Space transportation includes all vessels and equipment designed to be used in and to travel to and from space. This category includes space ports, space stations and space borne shipyards. Please note that space related activities will be covered in the Exodus Project book.

PART III
MAKING THE DREAM
A REALITY

INTRODUCTION

The Genesis Project is our plan to recreate society, establish communities and cities, and eventually to establish a new planet wide nation. The point of this is to bring the power back to the people and to create a society that we hope will, one day, bring an end to greed, corruption, war and suffering. We are somewhat limited in how we may pursue becoming a state because every piece of land in existence today has already been taken and claimed by some other state. Therefore, the only real option we have available to us, short of outright conflict which we are ill prepared to sustain, is to work within each nation-state and its established systems, systematically altering them bit by bit until we bring them into alignment with our vision for the future. The method of alteration is the Genesis Project.

The Genesis Project may be carried out in six primary phases. These primary phases should be considered as long-term goals and have been broken down into a series of objectives which should, with the exception of a few of the objectives, be considered as short-term goals, the achievement of which would complete a phase.

PHASE I
COMMUNITY PLANNING

OBJECTIVE 1: COMMUNICATION

Communication is the first step in the process of community planning and continues to be ongoing regardless of whatever phase we may be working in at any given time. It entails the sharing of ideas, of concerns and a lot of brainstorming. Special attention should be given to the discussion of the following subjects:

- Agriculture
- Building & Construction
- Community Events
- Economy
- Education & Culture
- Emergency Services & Public Safety
- Employment
- Homes & Living Space
- Parks & Recreation
- Public Health
- Renewable Energy & Resources
- Transportation
- Waste Management

A forum has been established in order to encourage and support communication regarding the Genesis Project. After having read this book you are encouraged to join the forum and participate in the discussions there. The URL is:

http://genesis-project.boards.net/

You may also find some useful information at the website of the Terran Empire:

http://www.terran-empire.us

CYBERIA

Cyberia is a city project like no other in the Genesis Project because it exists primarily in cyberspace. One of the primary functions of Cyberia is communication. It would be necessary to have the officers of the Terran Empire working together in the same local area in order to better facilitate communication and to coordinate efforts. Originally this was in-tended to mean in the same physical location. Cyberia will meet this requirement in cyberspace, allowing communication in the same non-physical location. This will allow the officers of the Terran Empire to exist in separate, even distant, physical locations while still meeting the requirement to work together locally. This holds true even for other members of the Terran Empire who wish to work together on various projects but who live distantly from one another. Aside from this, Cyberia has potential as a virtual social network and educational platform for the members of the Terran Empire.

Today, Cyberia exists only as a section of the Genesis Project forum. This is Cyberia in its infancy yet it still meets the basic requirements for communication. As more interest builds in the city of Cyberia it will become possible, eventually, for Cyberia to manifest in cyberspace as a world in virtual reality.

Cyberia is a platform where we may connect with others regardless of wherever we may live on the planet. It is important to remember that we, as a people, are a nation even if we do not yet have a state. The definition of "nation" is: "a people who share common customs, origins, history and frequently a language; a nationality." As mem-bers of the Terran Empire we are one people and all of these things will become common to us. We are a nation scattered across the planet without a state but our common home is our planet, Earth. You can discuss Cyberia on the following board:

http://genesis-project.boards.net/board/34/city-cyberia

CLASSIFICATIONS

When considering the building of a community we need to classify our various areas of concern in order to establish a reasonable plan of action. This plan of action may also be applied to building our cities.

The classification system we will use will be based on a three-tier system of classification as follows:

- General Classification
- Detailed Classification
- Usage or Facilities

These classifications will help us to understand how we need to designate areas and resources in our communities although how these areas are arranged will differ from community to community. Please see table II-1 on page 65.

DOMESTIC

Residential

Within the residential classification we have the concern of living space and agriculture. These apply to both the house and the commonwealth.

Living space is one of the most important aspects of our project. It is important because of the population requirements that we must meet in order to incorporate as a city. We simply cannot ask others to move to our communities without providing adequate living space for them. Dwellings will be constructed as funds permit and will be simple but practical. Once a dwelling has been completed, an individual or family who supports the project will be invited to move in. The dwelling will remain the property of the community and in order for the individual or family

TABLE II – 1

GENERAL	DETAILED	USAGE / FACILITIES/DIVISIONS
Domestic	Residential	Dwellings
		Agriculture
	Commercial	Business to Consumer
	Industrial	Primary
		Secondary
		Tertiary
		Quaternary
	Culture & Education	Schools
		Libraries
		Museums
		Educational Parks
	Parks & Recreation	Sports Facilities
		Green Spaces
		Hiking Trails
		Biking Trails
		Pet Parks
		Playgrounds
	Public Health & Safety	Emergency Services
		Hospitals
		Clinics

to remain in the community and continue living in the dwelling they must contribute to the community on a regular and as needed basis. Residents will be provided with several options in how they may contribute to the enrichment and expansion of the community. All properties remain common property of the people however in the case of dwellings they are assigned for the specific use of an individual or family. This arrangement relieves the individual of the burden of taxes on the property and gives the community greater latitude when the community needs to be reorganized. This arrangement will be carried over into our cities whereby the residential districts are owned in common by the people but are assigned to the exclusive use of a family or commonwealth.

The initial dwellings will be very basic consisting of bedrooms, bathrooms, kitchens, dining rooms and living rooms. In the future, however, dwellings will be organized into apartments and the buildings in which they are placed will follow definite modular plans.

Residential districts will be assigned to houses or commonwealths, both of which are responsible for agricultural production.

Commercial

All businesses, whether general store, restaurant, or some other type of business, will be organized under a single managing entity of the government. People will use their earned labor-time credits in these businesses to obtain goods and services.

Commercial districts may be zoned as to the type of businesses that may be operated within the district.

Industrial

Defined, industry "is the production of a good or service within an economy," and can be generally divided into five sectors: primary, secondary, tertiary, quaternary and quinary.

Culture & Education

This category includes schools, museums, libraries, educational parks and other educational and cultural facilities.

Education will play a large role in how our culture develops.

Parks & Recreation

There are many types of parks and recreational facilities that may be utilized within our cities. These provide an environment of relaxation, fun, exercise and entertainment.

Public Health & Safety

This category includes medical facilities such as hospitals and clinics, health departments, and emergency services such as police, security, fire and ambulance services. This category may also include Community Emergency Response (CERT) teams. Once incorporated the city may establish training facilities to train emergency services personnel. Law enforcement training includes various areas such as security, law enforcement and investigations. These courses would be included in Branch Specific Training (BST) of the Police Division.

OBJECTIVE 2: RECRUITING

Recruiting is the next objective in phase I and is an essential operation because the project, without people, is useless. The people are what make the project work and are absolutely vital to its success.

As with communication, recruiting will be ongoing. We will be generally open minded about recruiting because we believe everyone can do something to help our cause. It is important, though, to target those with specialized skills who, through the use of their skills, can help us to achieve our goals. Discussions will be required to determine more specifically what skills will be the most beneficial in the beginning.

An important part of the recruiting process will be to establish a presence on the internet. Once enough members have been recruited from our online presence we will start to establish local chartered units. These local units may then begin their own local recruiting operations through various local activities. Our invitations to relocate to our communities will be extended first to members we have recruited into the Terran Empire.

OBJECTIVE 3: FUNDING

Because we live in a primarily capitalist world we must operate within the capitalist system until we bring ourselves to a point where we are no longer required to do so. Therefore, funding will be pretty much central to everything we want to accomplish and is one of the most crucial aspects of the project. Fundraising will always be an ongoing process and we must be creative in discovering ways to obtain funding in support of our projects.

FUNDING SOURCE #1: DONATIONS

The Terran Empire will accept donations from any source provided they are "no strings attached" donations. We will not cater to any special interest as a prerequisite for a donation. Donations may or may not be tax deductible depending on our status at the time the donation is being made.

FUNDING SOURCE #2: IMPERIAL COOPERATIVE

Our institutions are intended to act as a shield between the world of capitalism and our people. This will be facilitated by the creation of the Imperial Cooperative. For now, however, the cooperative may serve the purpose to aid in funding the Terran Empire and in implementing our projects. Since the members of the cooperatives earn labor-time credits (LTC's), any money the cooperative earns as a profit over the cost of doing business can be used in many beneficial ways. For example, we can build homes for our people at no cost to them, where the cooperative members are given the first chance at having one of these homes. The money can also be used to build our administrative buildings and any other kind of building we need. It can be used to purchase land and property for Terran Empire uses (to build these homes and buildings, for example). And it can be used to provide free services to our people. The list of what we can do can go on but providing for the basic needs of our people are at the top of the list.

In the future, when we have established our first municipal government, this cooperative will take on the function of shield between our people and the capitalist world. Any excess product of any type produced within our city may be traded or sold through the cooperative. Any profit the cooperative realizes may then be used toward the benefit of the people and the community. This will also allow us to obtain needed resources that we cannot otherwise obtain within our own borders. We might also be able to provide a selection of products not otherwise readily available to our people within our communities.

As we expand our borders to include more cities, counties and, eventually states, this cooperative will serve them all.

OBJECTIVE 4: GENERAL COMMUNITY PLANNING AND LAND SEARCHING

General community planning consists of very general and basic planning. It also includes searching for land that is suitable for establishing our community. Ideally it should be located close to a local source of water. Once land has been located that is suitable, more specific and detailed community planning can occur.

PHASE II
OBTAIN LAND AND EQUIPMENT

OBJECTIVE 1: OBTAIN LAND

We will have to obtain land before any real progress can be made. Once the land has been obtained, the real work begins. Once we have the funds, after finding suitable land for our community, we make the land purchase. The primary purpose in obtaining land is to establish a community where people are brought together into one local area. This will make work and communication much easier. It is also necessary to have a certain amount of registered voters in one local area to make incorporation of a city possible.

The land will become useful in fundraising efforts through the hosting of private and some public events. Admission will be charged for some of those events and these funds will assist us in present and future objectives.

OBJECTIVE 2: OBTAIN EQUIPMENT

Having obtained land we must start to obtain the required equipment to prepare the land for community building operations. The land must be surveyed so that we can determine how to allocate areas for use. For example: living space, shipping and receiving operations, special events areas, etc.

OBJECTIVE 3: ESTABLISH WORK TEAMS

Initially a caretaker would be appointed to care for the land obtained that would take care of the initial preparations for the arrival of work teams. The caretaker would ensure that the land has been surveyed and a location for the caretaker's dwelling would then be chosen. The caretaker would then take steps to secure the parameters of the property. The caretaker must work with the officers of the Terran Empire to determine where the center of the community will be located so that community planning can take place around the center of the community. The community plan should include a community management area in the center, dwellings, a small medical facility, a school, a postal facility, an entrance processing facility, shopping areas and a community parking area for those who own vehicles and must find income outside of the community. These vehicles would not be allowed in the community.

Members who desire to reside in the community will be organized into various work teams and deployed to the site chosen for the community to begin land preparation and construction operations. Most, if not all, team members will become immediate residents of the community.

OBJECTIVE 4: LAND PREPARATION

During this objective the land will be cleared and leveled. The land excavated will be moved to a designated raw materials holding area for use later as needed. Whatever utility lines may be needed will be placed and roads will be established. The initial buildings for temporary living space will be built during this objective as well. Initially the caretaker will start this work but will be joined by work teams later to complete it.

Some of the first structures built may be temporary and may only provide the very basic essentials for survival although they need not be primitive. The first structures will necessarily be dwellings, storage areas and a workshop. The workshop will be where construction materials will be prepared for use.

OBJECTIVE 5: ESTABLISH COOPERATIVE

In this objective we establish a cooperative organization which will be the first step in producing for the needs of the community. Any excess will be exported through a market established by the Terran Empire in order to obtain funds for our projects and needs which generally are those things we cannot yet do or provide for ourselves. Even those who create various works of art or crafts may participate in the cooperative and market.

PHASE III
COMMUNITY BUILDING

OBJECTIVE 1: CONSTRUCTION

During this phase our work teams will concentrate on the building of facilities necessary for the function of government, economy, production and apartments. The apartments will be for those individuals and families who take an active hands-on role in building the community to a point where we will be able to incorporate as a city.

Besides homes, the following facilities will initially be required:

- Community administration buildings
- A school
- A clinic
- Work buildings
- Community gardens

OBJECTIVE 2: INDIVIDUAL & FAMILY RELOCATION

During this phase we start relocating individuals and families to an intake processing area for the community. All adult community members would be required to register to vote due to the fact that this is one of the key requirements for incorporating the community as a city. They would also be required to abide by community rules and to take an active role in building and maintaining the community and its works. This requirement can be satisfied by joining and participating in the Imperial Cooperatives.

PHASE IV
CITY PLANNING

OBJECTIVE 1: ASSESS THE BASIC NEEDS OF THE COMMUNITY

In this objective we simply determine what each city will need in the beginning and use this information later in the city planning objective. Things such as education, employment, transportation, basic city services, public health and safety and utilities are all examples of what might be discussed during this objective.

As with the first objective of Phase I we will use a three-tiered classification system to help determine our plan of action. Again, we will use the following three categories:

- General Classification
- Detailed Classification
- Usage or facilities

Table II – 3 on page 75 should help to give you an idea of how these categories are organized.

OBJECTIVE 2: CITY PLANNING

In this objective we use what we have established in objective 1. The three primary concerns in this objective are governance, living space and jobs. Each city will be composed of 9 townships arranged in a 3 township x 3 township grid. Each township will be 6 miles on each side creating a township of 36 square miles and a city of 324 square miles (not including the green spaces between the townships or the roads between the districts). Each town-

GENERAL	DETAILED	USAGE / FACILITIES/DIVISIONS
City Districts	Residential	House/Hold
		Commonwealth
	Commercial	Various Business Types
	Industrial	Food Processing
		Construction Materials
		Textiles Plants
		Pharmaceutical Plants
		Fuel Production Plants
	Government	Hospitals/Clinics/ Bioresearch/Veterinary Medicine
		Public Safety & Security
		Education/Cultural
		General Utilities
		Transportation & Supply

TABLE II – 3

ship will be divided from one another by a one district wide green space on each side.

Each township will be divided into four wards comprised of 36 districts each. A township will also be composed of 36 sectors each of which is 1 square mile. Sectors will be divided into districts each of which is 1/2 mile on each side or 1/4 square mile (160 acres).

Diagram Fig. II-1 on page 76 illustrates the basic township layout. Each square within the township represents a district. The shaded areas surrounding the township indicate green space for recreation and/or wild-life areas.

Each district will be assigned a zoning classification of which there are four types:

- Administration
- Residential
- Commercial
- Industrial

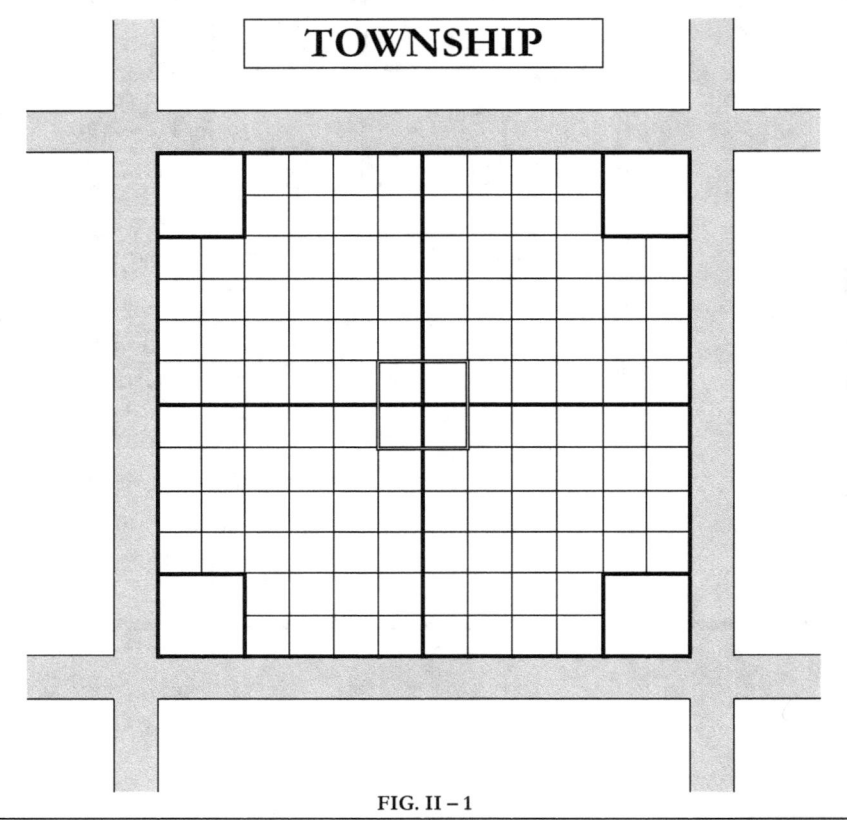

FIG. II – 1

Townships will be composed mostly of residential districts which will provide living space and a place to raise families. They will also provide agricultural product for use to industry or to government for export. Administration districts will provide employment, governance and certain services. Commercial districts will provide employment, entertainment, services and shopping. Industrial districts will provide employment and whatever is needed by any of the other districts. The larger districts in each corner of the township diagram above are commonwealth districts. Commonwealth districts might look something like the cities designed by Jacque Fresco of the Venus Project on the following page.

Many of the designs of Jacque Fresco can be applied in the Genesis Project and are discussed in his book "**The Best that Money Can't Buy: Beyond Politics, Poverty and War**" The book can be purchased on the Venus Project website:

http://thevenusproject.com/store/official#!/~/product/id=5501756

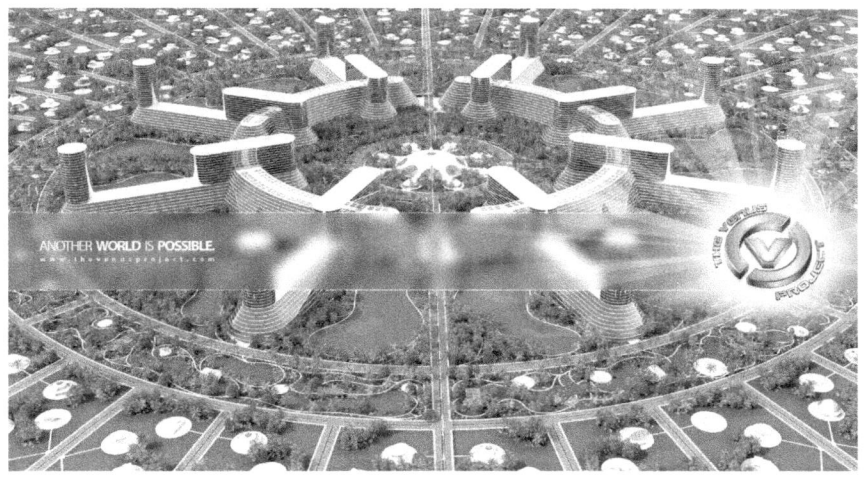

http://www.thevenusproject.com

ROADS AND TRANSPORTATION

Each district will be bordered by roads that will be used by government, public safety, agricultural and utility vehicles. It is intended that our cities remain car free for the most part. Transportation between the districts will be via free public transportation, bike or walking. Public transportation will be via monorail with monorail stations located at each district center.

Secured parking decks will be established at the city borders for citizens who own vehicles and use them outside of the city, although we do hope to eventually eliminate this need.

THE DISTRICTS

There will be four kinds of districts within our cities according to how they have been zoned. Each district will be composed of two to three areas as follows (Fig. II-2 below):

- District Center
- District General Use Area
- Green Space

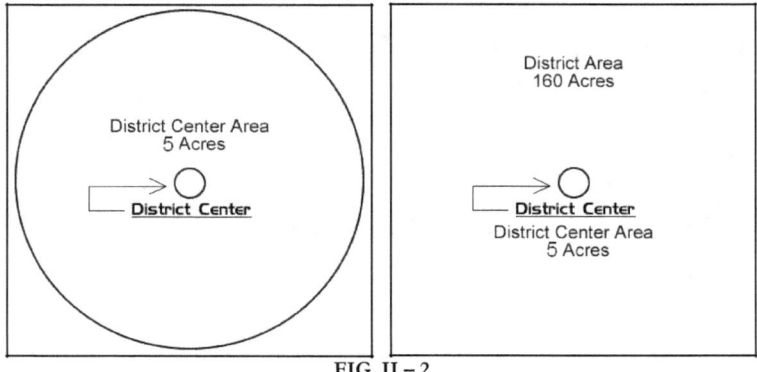

FIG. II – 2

Not all districts will include the green space but most will. The green spaces are intended to balance development and wild habitat providing space for wildlife. Each township will also be bordered by green space on each side for the same reason. The bordering natural space between townships may be developed for recreation, as with promenades or parks, provided that they do not detract from the primary purpose of providing a habitat for the wild, or necessity, or it may remain undeveloped depending on the environment.

The districts are designed in such a way that each point in the district may be reached by walking or riding a bike. Again, travel between the districts is accomplished via public transportation although nothing would prohibit walking or riding a bike between the districts.

Residential Districts

A residential district includes all three district areas and serves two primary functions:

- Residential space for citizens
- Agricultural production

Each house or commonwealth is assigned a specific residential district unless it grows so large that it overpopulates the district. When a house begins to exceed its population limits it may be assigned additional residential districts. When a commonwealth reaches its population limits volunteers may establish a new commonwealth which will then be assigned to a new residential district.

The dwellings for the house or commonwealth and the monorail station for the district are located at the district center. The district center will be organized into concentric rings of spacious apartments. Apartments will be grouped into buildings that are separated from one another by open spaces. These open spaces may be enclosed through the use of atriums that will allow for practical landscaping with plants that will provide both food and medicine. The residential district general use area is used for agricultural purposes and is managed by the house or commonwealth members occupying the district. These agricultural areas may be used for raising crops or livestock.

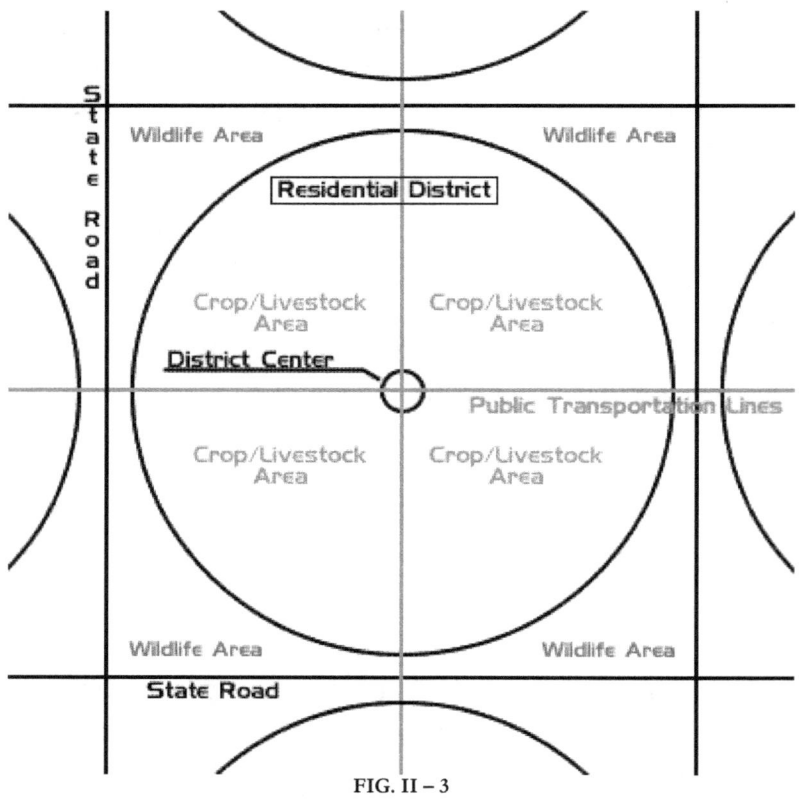

FIG. II – 3

Because the house and commonwealth are responsible for agricultural operations, the larger the family or commonwealth the better. In very large families or commonwealths not all members will be required to assist the house or commonwealth in fulfilling its agricultural obligations. The larger they are, the less of a burden is placed upon each individual member.

Administration Districts

Administrative districts may or may not include green spaces and are assigned for administrative use and management including uses such as administration, education, medicine, corrections, public safety, public health, research and development, etc.

The district center of an administrative district serves as a staging area for the rest of the district for public transportation, public safety and emergency response, post and parcel operations and general distribution of materials. Administrative operations take place outside the district center for the most part.

Ideally each administrative district will be zoned for one primary function although in the beginning stages of city building, out of necessity, a single administrative district may be assigned several functions.

Commercial districts

Commercial districts will be managed by the cooperative and will include all three district areas. These districts are the center of commerce and business and might include shopping malls, restaurants, office buildings, entertainment related businesses or any combination of these.

Industrial Districts

Industrial districts will also be managed by the cooperative and may or may not include green space. These districts are where products are made and where materials are processed. Industrial districts supply all of the other districts with the products and materials they need to remain in business or to continue operating.

Currently the Terran Empire has classified industrial operations as follows:

- Manufacturing
- Distribution
- Waste management
- Construction

Intake Processing Districts

The intake processing districts play an important role in the migration of new citizens to our cities. They are established to facilitate intake and orientation of new citizens. These districts will consist of apartments, schools, community service facilities and any other facilities to address the needs of citizens in this district.

Individuals and couples who have completed the orientation process, but who do not meet the eligibility requirements to form a house will be relocated to a public housing district or may be offered the opportunity to join one of the commonwealths.

Families that have completed the orientation process will either be organized as a house and relocated to a residential district or will be given the opportunity to join one of the commonwealths. If a residential district is not available the house will be relocated to a public housing district and placed on a waiting list until a residential district becomes available. The first house on the list will be relocated to the first available residential district.

As citizens are relocated from the intake processing district to residential or public housing districts new families and individuals will take their place.

Public Housing Districts

Public housing districts will be established for couples and individuals who are not attached to a house or commonwealth and who do not meet the eligibility requirements for forming a house. If their status changes so that they are eligible to form a house and wish to do so, they will be relocated to a residential district if one is available. If a residential district is not available, the house will be placed on a waiting list with other houses until a residential district does become available.

PHASE V
INCORPORATION

OBJECTIVE 1: STUDY LEGAL REQUIREMENTS

In this objective we must study and gain an understanding of the legal requirements for incorporating a city in the local area where the community exists. An understanding of these laws will be required for the next objective.

OBJECTIVE 2: INCORPORATION PREPARATION

Once we have achieved the required population of registered voters and after having studied the legal requirements as mentioned in objective 1, we must use those legal requirements as our guide in preparing the required fees and documents for incorporation. It is important to know which documents are needed, what is required for their completion, to what official or agency they must be submitted and how much it will cost. We must then do what is necessary to prepare the documents and raise the funds to pay the required fees.

OBJECTIVE 3: INCORPORATE

In this objective we submit our prepared documents and the required fees to the appropriate officials and/or agencies. This objective is important because, as a city, we will have achieved very real political authority, even if on a small scale. Over time, however, this authority can and will grow.

As a city we will have the ability to acquire new territory through annexation and eminent domain, to train law enforcement and CERT teams, to enact and enforce laws and to establish various other functions of government. We will also have the ability to establish various social programs for our people.

OBJECTIVE 4: FORM CITY ADMINISTRATION

After having incorporated we must form the city administration according to local laws. However, ideally the city administration should be formed in the following man-ner.

First, a city council should be appointed by citizens. It shall have authority to oversee the general operations of the city. The city council should be no fewer than three members and no greater than 9 depending on the number of townships that exist within the city. When all nine townships exist in a city there will be nine council members. The number of council members, however, should always be an odd number. Generally, each township is composed of four wards. An alderman will be appointed by the citizens for each ward. From the four aldermen one person will be appointed by the citizens as the city councilman for that township.

Second, the citizens should appoint from among the city council members a mayor who will be the presiding member of the city council.

Third, the city council should appoint a city manager who will oversee the administrative and executive operations of the city and advise the council.

Fourth, municipal judges will be appointed by the citizens.

Fifth, other city posts will be filled such as: city attorney, city clerk, etc.

OBJECTIVE 5: INITIAL APPOINTMENTS

During this objective the citizens will appoint the members of the city council and other city officials through a special voting process.

OBJECTIVE 6: ESTABLISH INITIAL ORDINANCES

In this objective the citizens will establish the initial city ordinances.

PHASE VI
CITY BUILDING, GROWTH & EXPANSION

OBJECTIVE 1: CITY BUILDING

In this objective we work to establish the first few districts of our city and build them up. The configuration may look something like the arrangement in FIG. II-4 below.

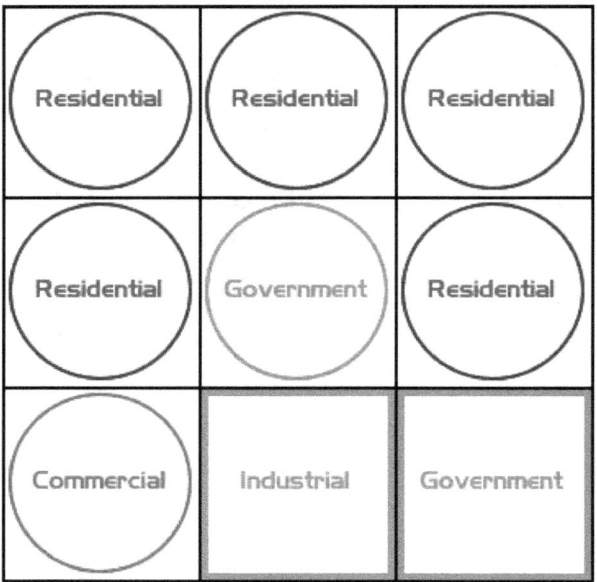

FIG. II – 4

OBJECTIVE 2: NEW CITIZEN INTAKE

In this objective we begin relocating new citizens to the intake processing districts for transitioning into our society.

OBJECTIVE 3: CITY GROWTH & EXPANSION

Once the first few districts have been established we must work to expand our city to complete one full township through a process of annexation and in some cases eminent domain. After having completed the first township we must work to complete the remaining town-ships to complete the city.

OBJECTIVE 4: SEEDING NEW CITIES

Once we have accomplished the task of building our first city we will work to seed new cities from the original one. Ideally, these will be planned and built the same manner as the first city using whatever we have learned from city building up to that point. Each city should ideally be seeded next to an existing city on a side where nothing exists, in keeping with the established grid system.

This is the way in which we will continue to build up our political influence and expand our territory. Our goal here is to keep expanding as much as possible. Expansion is important because it is through expansion that we will acquire more living space for our people and how we will acquire new resources.

AFTERWARD

As you've read through this work no doubt you may have noticed a familiarity with some of the works of popular science fiction of our day. It is true that I am a fan of the science fiction genre. You see, the works of science fiction come from the great imaginations of their creators and in many ways represent the hopes, dreams and vision of what could be. Sometimes they also represent the fears and concerns about some of these possibilities. And while it is also true that some parts of these works of science fiction are pure fantasy, others are quite doable in our reality provided the proper attention and effort is applied to a given subject. Therefore I believe we should take from the best of these works and apply them to some of the situations and problems we are faced with today to help us build a better tomorrow for our children and for the common good of all.

Please understand that I make no claims to being a professional author. It was purely my intent to share with you my vision for the future. Having limited means, I have edited this work to the best of my ability. Please forgive any misspellings and grammatical errors and do not allow them to distract you from the spirit and purpose of this work. Should you happen to find any errors (remember that this book is written in American English, not the Queen's English) feel free to e-mail me at: **scott.yancey@terran-empire.us** citing the location and nature of the error along with your suggested correction.

APPENDICES

APPENDIX A
HOW TO ESTABLISH A HOUSE &
HOLD -OR- A COMMONWEALTH

THE HOUSE & HOLD

It should be understood that the house and hold apply to families with children who are genetically related. If you are a single individual or a couple without children and you do not already belong to an existing house, you may either apply to join an existing commonwealth or register a commonwealth and get others to join you. It should also be noted that families with children who are genetically related are not required to register a house. They may also apply to join a commonwealth or register one as with single individuals or couples without children.

The following steps apply primarily to people who live in the United States. People living in other countries can adapt and modify the steps according to what may be dictated by circumstances.

THE FIRST STEP

The first step to establish a house for those families who meet the requirements is to register its charter with the Terran Empire. It is required that the house take on the surname of the person who is registering it. For example, Scott Yancey founded the House of Yancey, the first registered house of the Terran Empire. If there is already an existing house with your existing surname and you are not a direct descendant of the person who registered that house, your house will be designated as "The 2nd, 3rd, 4th, etc. House of…" as determined by the Terran Empire. For example, if Tom Yancey were to register a house charter and Tom is not a direct descendant of Scott, then Tom's house would be named "The 2nd House of Yancey." Tom and Scott may be related, perhaps cousins for example, but not direct descendants of one another with no house established in their ancestry to bring them under one charter instead of two separate ones.

In some cases a single parent may establish a house for the sake of their children. You should become familiar with the current rules regarding house registration and how they apply to your circumstances.

In the charter you will need to designate the name of your first clan. It may not be the same as the surname of your house or any other existing house or clan registered under the Terran Empire. A good choice for a clan name would be to name it after a descriptive object that holds meaning for your family. For example, the first clan established in the House of Yancey is the Blackstar Clan. The black star has a special symbolic meaning to the House of Yancey.

The house and clan may be established as "holdless" meaning that it has no land upon which a permanent home can be established. If, for example, your family must rent an apartment, live with other family or friends, or are one of the unfortunate families that are homeless, you would be registering as a holdless house and clan. This may change, of course, and hopefully for you and your family it does. When it does this land, even if just a house with a small yard, becomes a hold that takes on the name of your clan. The House of Yancey and the Blackstar Clan started out as holdless, having to both rent and endure homelessness for long periods of time. Now the House of Yancey has land designated as Blackstar Hold. So, even if you must register your house and clan as holdless, keep hope! Know that even as the House of Yancey was able to do it so can you. Your family can rise above holdlessness even from the depths of homelessness if you allow the Terran Empire to guide you.

If your family already has land upon which a permanent home can be built or which already exists, upon registration of your house and clan it becomes a hold and takes on the name of your clan in the form of "[Clan name] Hold." For example, the Blackstar Clan now holds Blackstar Hold.

In order to register a house you must be a member/citizen of the Terran Empire and you must be able to prove the identity of the house members and provide some basic information. The Terran Empire will formulate your house charter and design the heraldic devices for your house and initial clan at no additional charge. You can use the heraldic devices immediately upon acceptance of your house and clan charter registration provided they are used in an appropriate manner.

THE HOLDLESS

For those who must register as holdless, it is imperative that you begin working toward establishing a hold for your family. Even if your family is homeless what we suggest here will help you.

If your life, or that of your family, is in disarray, it is not likely that you will be organized enough to do anything constructive for our cause or for your own. Therefore, in order to change that there are three things you must do: Practice discipline and focused intent, put your life back in order and begin to build an intellectual understanding about what we are trying to do and why we are trying to do it.

Putting your life back in order is the first step and does take discipline to accomplish. However, you can use this first step to help you strengthen your discipline and learn to focus your intent by practicing the commitment to do or not to do something each day. Focus on doing positive things that help you to reach your goals and on not doing the negative things that will keep you from achieving them. The time to begin this first step is **RIGHT NOW**! Your focus and concern must be toward establishing a stable lifestyle through having a way of making a living, eliminating debts without incurring more debt, and fulfilling obligations without creating more obligation. Doing these things will help you to provide balance and clarity in your life and will free you to pursue your goals.

THE SECOND STEP

The second step entails obtaining land upon which a permanent home can be built. This step will be much easier for you and your family to accomplish if at least some of the members in your family are employable, can drive a vehicle and have transportation. The Terran Empire can provide your family with information on where land can be purchased at low prices. It should come as no surprise that many of these parcels of land will be located in the same local areas. This is in keeping with establishing comm- unities in the same local areas to build up a like-minded population, grow our political influence in the area and finally to begin the process of city incorporation per the Genesis Project.

If you already have land upon which a permanent home can be built or that already exists you can skip this step and move on to the third step. You do not need to relocate to one of the areas mentioned above although you would have a greater advantage than those who have nothing. The money obtained from the sale of your current property could purchase one of these land parcels outright and get you well on the way to development of your land parcel. Otherwise it's perfectly acceptable to keep what you have and work toward the goals of the Genesis Project right where you are.

Your family might also work on obtaining and becoming familiar with some of the symbols of your house and clan during this time. These include the home stones, family chest, and family altar and associated items. The home stones, one for the house and one for the clan, represent the stability and longevity of your family as it is perpetuated through time. The family chest and family altar are focuses of family celebrations and a place to remember your ancestors, as memorials. Ancestor worship is not implied here unless that is part of your family tradition or belief. Likewise, the family altar has no religious or spiritual significance unless your family ascribes them to your family alter. Generally it is meant to serve as a place where family achievements may be displayed.

THE THIRD STEP

The third step entails developing your land parcel and becoming more involved in local Terran Empire affairs so that your family becomes more invested and rooted in the local community. Establishing a local cooperative as described in this book is an important aspect of your community involvement. So if the hold of your family exists in an area close to other holds and commonwealths, part of your involvement in the community should be working toward establishing a cooperative and managing it to the greater good of the people thereafter. One valuable function of this cooperative is that it can assist your hold as well as other holds and commonwealths in the area with the development of your and their land parcels, among other things.

If you've bought any of the properties suggested by the Empire chances are there are no services or utilities to the property. This is one of the reasons that many of the properties have such a low price. Part of developing your land means that you establish these services and utilities for yourself either by yourself or with the help of a cooperative. Even if you already own property or a home with utilities and services you can still work to go "off grid" and become more self-sufficient.

If there is no home on your property you might live in a temporary type of shelter while building your permanent home. Some people might elect to utilize tents, sheds, camper trailers, RV's or mobile homes and moving into the permanent home while still building it as soon as it is safe to do so. Each temporary shelter has advantages and disadvantages depending on the local laws, local terrain, local climate and personal preference.

Another area you'll need to work on while developing your land is preparing it to grow plants and livestock to use both as food and to use at the local Imperial Cooperative if one exists. What you should grow and what animals you raise depends on what you can grow based on your local climate and also on what your family will actually eat.

THE COMMONWEALTH

A commonwealth may be registered by any adult member/citizen of the Terran Empire who is not already a member of an existing house or commonwealth, unless that member intends to separate from that existing house or commonwealth. Commonwealths are registered in order to provide an alternative form of community to that of the house and is complete in and of itself without the additional designations of hold or clan. As with the clan, however, the registered name of the commonwealth should be based on a descriptive object that is secular in nature and that represents the theme of the commonwealth. The form that the name of the commonwealth will take is "[Chosen name] Commonwealth." The steps to establishing the commonwealth firmly in the community are generally the same as that of the house.

APPENDIX B
ESTABLISHING AN IMPERIAL COOPERATIVE

INTRODUCTION

Imperial Cooperatives will become a very important part of the Genesis and Exodus projects and of the various city projects that will exist under them. It will be through the cooperatives that labor and production are managed either through central planning or through the determination of the workers depending on what is being produced. Both types of cooperatives are intended to exist simultaneously.

The primary purpose of the cooperatives is to facilitate the implementation of the Genesis and Exodus projects and to meet the basic needs of our people. The three primary basic needs of our people are food/water/medicine, shelter and clothing. The need for safety and security is met, in part, by the fulfillment of the need for shelter. Therefore, each cooperative established should have the fulfillment of these needs as its primary objective. Outside of these primary objectives a cooperative may participate in any industry it feels is necessary.

On the following pages we discuss the top three objectives and then we will discuss the steps necessary to establish a Imperial Cooperative.

OBJECTIVE 1: WATER, FOOD AND MEDICINE

The first objective of any Imperial Cooperative should be to establish systems and services whereby water, food and medicines are provided for our people. The first concern within this objective is the need for water because water is absolutely necessary for life. On average a person can only go for about three days without water before they die. Water is a vital need to human life. Additionally, without water we cannot raise any kind of livestock or crops for food or medicines.

In places where water rights are restricted through law we must work to change those laws to the benefit of the people.

Cooperatives might work toward obtaining water well drilling rigs so that the cooperatives can drill wells where this is a viable option, assist home owners with setting up water catchment systems for collecting the runoff from rain or snow or to even provide services to haul water into where it is needed. When the need for water can be met the cooperatives can move on to the concern for food.

Food comes to us from two sources: animals and plants. One of the best ways for a cooperative to produce food is for its members to produce it individually on their own property. Individual members cannot only produce enough food for themselves but also some excess additional food that can be brought to the cooperative markets and café and used as previously described under the section in this book regarding cooperatives. Those who were unable to produce enough for their families or who were unable to produce a particular item may be able to supplement their supplies through the cooperative market. The cooperative market would become an excellent resource for the exchange of seeds and plants among our people. Some seeds and plants would be common while others may be rare. Those that are rare would become less so as more people grow them and continue to exchange them in the market.

OBJECTIVE 2: SHELTER & BUILDING CONSTRUCTION

The second objective of the cooperative should be to set up facilities that produce materials for the construction of buildings and shelter. The cooperative should also provide construction services as it is able. For members of the cooperative, the construction of buildings and the materials produced by the cooperative for construction would be free of charge provided they are utilized to meet the basic needs of those they are being constructed for. Members would use their labor time credits for any other types of buildings. Non-members of the cooperative would pay a low cost for those materials and services.

OBJECTIVE 3: CLOTHING & TEXTILE PRODUCTION

The third objective of the cooperative should be to establish facilities for the production of clothing and textiles from natural renewable fibers such as cotton, hemp and wool. While clothing would be free to our members other textiles would be available through purchase using their labor-time credits. Both clothing and textiles would be available to non-members for a low cost.

STARTING THE IMPERIAL COOPERATIVE

If you are interested in starting an Imperial Cooperative you will want to have a few others who are also interested in starting it with you who will take an active role in helping the cooperative succeed. At the very least you will need two other people, preferably more, besides yourself to start the cooperative.

If your cooperative is small and you are starting with just a few people who've never been involved with a cooperative before you may want to start with doing simple things like growing food to share within the cooperative or using your skills to help others within the cooperative in various ways. Your cooperative will want to work toward bringing in new members so that as the cooperative grows it will have the ability to do more and offer more services to its members. Eventually the cooperative may begin to offer services and products to non-members for a much lower cost than they could find elsewhere.

In time the cooperative members will learn and begin to understand the benefits of the cooperative as well as some possible pitfalls and how to deal with them. Keep in mind that your new cooperative should be working toward accomplishing the goals and objectives as they have been discussed in previous pages.

STEP ONE: LEARN

Before starting a Imperial Cooperative you will want to learn as much as you can about existing cooperatives and how they operate so that you can apply what you've learned once you have started your cooperative. You might learn through direct experience within an existing cooperative if one is available in your local area. Or you might learn indirectly through various media types that exist on the internet. In the latter case you may wish to take advantage of search engines to search for information about cooperatives, blogs and forums that discuss cooperatives or through watching videos about cooperatives.

STEP TWO: DISCUSS

The second step would be to discuss starting an Imperial Cooperative with people you know. Perhaps family, friends and in some cases people you may be acquainted with or know professionally. It is ok if some of these people aren't interested. If they aren't don't push the issue with them. Just let it be, bring the idea to others, and concentrate more on those who show an interest in the cooperative idea. Those who have a genuine intent to help will show it by their actions. Spend most of your time and effort with the people who are actually participating.

STEP THREE: FORM THE COOPERATIVE

In this step you will officially form the cooperative with those others who have come together to work together within the cooperative. This is accomplished first by registering your cooperative with the Terran Empire.

APPENDIX C
DISTRICT DEVELOPMENT

INTRODUCTION

The first step in the development of a district is to know how the district has been zoned. This is important because the zoning will determine the types of buildings that will be allowed in a given district. In this appendix we will cover some of the issues related to developing the various districts.

GENERAL DEVELOPMENT

In most cases there are certain activities that occur in the development of a district that are common to most, if not all districts. For example, when any district is zoned the first step will be to send out specialized teams to prepare the land and begin construction. These common issues will be covered in this section.

MONORAIL

One of the first services to be established within a district will be the monorail lines and monorail station that will serve the district. This will enable many workers to reach the site easier. Once these are in place the rest of the buildings are built around this monorail hub.

The monorail hub will allow transport of people, products, mail, packages and other materials. Postal functions will originate at the monorail hub where mail will be accepted and transported or received and distributed throughout the district to its appropriate destination. Additionally, other areas may be included in the monorail hub for shopping, dining, recreation and entertainment.

COMMON DEVELOPMENT OF INDUSTRIAL, COMMERCIAL & GOVERNMENT DISTRICTS

After the monorail hub in these district types have been established pedestrian streets for use by bicycles and pedestrians will be laid out and construction will commence, as needed filling in the spaces. These streets will be laid out in concentric rings and the buildings of the inner rings will be built before the buildings of the outer rings.

THE RESIDENTIAL DISTRICT

As has been stated, commonwealths and houses will be assigned to the residential districts, which serve three primary purposes: living space, social space and agricultural production. Crop areas are a designated part of the design and layout of the residential district.

UTILITY CENTERS

In the residential district, after the monorail hub has been established, construction will begin on the utility centers. There are three primary utility centers in the construction. The first utility center houses the equipment needed to store and distribute electricity, water, and gas to the rest of the district. The second utility center houses equipment for media communications and is a communications hub and the third utility center houses the security and fire monitoring equipment.

There are three types of utility centers associated with the dwelling spaces of the hold. These would generally be separated from one another and are as follows:

- General utilities
- Waste utilities
- Communications & systems

The general utilities center manages the water supply, electricity and gas utilities. Essentially this utility center is configured so that water can produce both gas and electricity for practical use besides just supplying water for normal water uses. Electricity can also be produced using various methods, as with solar and wind power generation. The batteries, inverters and all other associated equipment would be located in this utility center.

The waste utility center generally deals primarily with liquid organic waste. Solid organic waste may be dealt with through composting, being turned into a fertilizer to be used on crops.

The communications & systems utility center is the communications and media hub of the district as well as the central hub for fire and security systems. Each apartment would be equipped with telephone/videophone systems, internet systems, media systems (Television and music) via cable and fiber optic connections, and fire and security related systems.

DWELLINGS

Dwellings in the residential district consist of apartments, the size of which depend on the size of the family or group being housed in them. Generally, a one bedroom apartment would be sufficient for an individual or couple. Two individuals who do not constitute a couple might be assigned a two bedroom. The amount of bedrooms will increase as the group or family size increases, up to 5 bedrooms and larger common space within the apartment. One area that may be missing from the apartment is the kitchen as there would be a common kitchen for the hold or the commonwealth. Occupants could either go to eat at the common dining room or have food delivered to the apartment. This would be a free access kitchen and labor-time credits would not have to be used to purchase food from these kitchens like it would be in a restaurant.

The buildings that house the dwellings will be modular so that as new apartments are needed they would simply be added to the structure. However, when a district has reached its limit of occupants, a new district would need to be assigned.

These apartment buildings will be arranged in concentric rings around the central monorail hub. And will extend out to the agricultural crop areas.

COMMON AREAS

Common areas consist of the pedestrian streets, kitchen and dining area, recreational centers, shopping areas, etc. that are not used as dwellings or for agricultural purposes. One of the important things about common areas is that they can also be used to grow produce. Whereas the agricultural fields are used to grow produce for the people for food consumption or industry, the common areas would be utilized to help grow food for the people of the house or commonwealth to supplement what can be obtained from the stores of the people. Urban gardening techniques can be used for this purpose. Instead of decorating the common areas with plants that really serve no purpose other than to look pretty, plants that produce food can be utilized in their place and in the landscaping of the various common areas. They can look good and produce something useful at the same time. These same plants can benefit from the use of aquaponics just as the agricultural areas can.

AGRICULTURAL AREAS

The monorail lines divide the residential district crop areas into four large sections. Each of these four sections can be utilized for planting crops or raising livestock. In the case of crops three of the areas can be planted while leaving the fourth fallow, or planting a nitrogen fixing crop such as clover. It may also be possible to institute a larger scale aquaponics system that would allow for all four fields to be planted each year providing food from both crops and from fish.

APPENDIX D
IMPERIAL NEW LIFE PROGRAM

INTRODUCTION

Here we outline a plan on how we intend to help those in need. This appendix applies primarily to helping the homeless.

THE PROGRAM

The Imperial New Life Program is intended primarily for those who are homeless although the program outline can also be adapted and utilized for those who want to transition out of their current situation into our homesteading program.

The program consists of four stages. Homelessness, while not a part of the program itself, is considered a stage that represents the condition of an individual or family before entering the program. As such, this condition has been designated as stage 0.

STAGE	CONDITION
0	Homelessness
1	Yancey House – Shelter
2	Yancey House – Transitional Housing
3	Imperial Communities
4	Homesteading Program

STAGE 1 – YANCEY HOUSE - SHELTER

Yancey House was named in honor of the founder of the Terran Empire and will be established to manage the first and second stages of the Imperial New Life Program. Stage 1 of the program is the initial stage where those homeless who have applied to enter the program undergo intake processing, orientation and familiarization with the program. In most cases, those who enter this stage will be unemployed for one reason or another. However, some who come into the program will be employed. In this case efforts must be made by program staff to work around the work schedules and job requirements of the program participants while still motivating them and working with them to ensure they continue working through the program. The requirements of the program should not place a participant's job in jeopardy. Having an income in these initial stages of the program is very important.

If participants come into the program unemployed, they will be asked to hold off on searching for employment until after the initial set of goals established for them by the program have been completed.

STAGE 2 – YANCEY HOUSE – TRANSITIONAL HOUSEING

This stage of the program is a transitional housing stage. During this stage program participants still have goals that must be achieved. Chief among these is preparing to re-enter regular social life. Whereas in stage 1 of the program the needs of the participants were primarily met by the program, in stage 2 participants will begin to take on more responsibility for themselves and their families through the use of skills that were learned in stage 1 of the program.

STAGE 3 – IMPERIAL COMMUNITIES

"Imperial Communities" refer to apartment buildings that are utilized in one of two ways. The first way is not directly part of the program. However the income obtained from the rent of the apartments of these buildings will be used to help fund the program.

The second way that the buildings are utilized is the same as the first way except that these buildings are also utilized as stage 3 of the program. In this third stage, program participants are moved out of the transitional housing of stage 2 into an apartment of their own in one of our communities. At this point they live pretty much like any other person who goes to work, pays bills, and takes care of their family.

In this stage participants are given a six month lease after which they may choose to continue on to stage 4 of the program, or exit the program by securing an apartment in one of our non-program buildings or by securing an apartment with another community. If the participants choose to continue on to stage 4 of the program their lease will automatically renew and may be ended by the program before the six month term is up if a place for the participant in stage 4 opens for them.

STAGE 4 – HOMESTEAD PROGRAM

In this stage participants obtain a homestead through the program in support of the Genesis and Exodus projects

PERSONAL NOTES & IDEAS

PERSONAL NOTES & IDEAS

PERSONAL NOTES & IDEAS

PERSONAL NOTES & IDEAS

www.ingramcontent.com/pod-product-compliance
Lightning Source LLC
Chambersburg PA
CBHW062009280526
45787CB00005B/2034

* 9 7 8 1 5 4 8 3 1 3 0 9 8 *